Teaching Comprehension Strategies

All Readers Need

by Nicole Outsen
and
Stephanie Yulga

SCHOLASTIC
PROFESSIONAL BOOKS

New York • Toronto • London • Auckland • Sydney • Mexico City
New Delhi • Hong Kong • Buenos Aires

We dedicate this book to our students,
the best teachers of all.

Acknowledgments

First, we extend our love and gratitude to Hindy List who offered us unwavering support, pushed us to become better teachers, and introduced us to Scholastic. Thanks also to Barbara Schneider who has given us, and so many other teachers, invaluable opportunities for professional growth. We must also thank the people of District 2 in New York City for creating an environment that allows teachers to share, reflect, and learn. We also want to thank Karen O'Neill, Rita Savur, Ellen Corcoran, Learning Through Teaching, and the fifth-grade team at North Hampton School for continually reminding us that teaching is learning.

At Scholastic, we thank Terry Cooper for giving us this amazing opportunity and Ray Coutu for his incredible knowledge, patience, and thoughtful feedback, without which this book wouldn't exist.

And, of course, we thank Zang, Andy, and our families for their long-suffering support. Yes, it's finally finished.

Cover design by James Sarfati
Interior design by Holly Grundon
Cover and interior photographs by Kevin Jacobus

ISBN 0-439-16514-8
Copyright © 2002 by Nicole Outsen and Stephanie Yulga
All rights reserved
Printed in the U.S.A.

Contents

Introduction

Early one morning, while having coffee and reviewing plans for the day, we agreed that our approach to reading was not working. We had had too many troubling reading conferences like this one between Nicole and one of her best readers:

Nicole: Kristen, how do you know you are understanding this *Junie B. Jones* book?

Kristen: I make lots of connections. When I don't understand what I'm reading, I re-read.

Wow, Nicole thought. *Kristen really gets it. She knows the importance of understanding what she reads and she's using strategies like making connections to help.* Nicole continued the conference.

Nicole: Can you show me an example—a place in this book where you made a connection or re-read when you didn't understand?

Kristen looked confused. She was unable to find one example.

Our third graders were not really *using* the comprehension strategies we had worked so hard to teach. They knew the vocabulary of those strategies. Fundamentally, they knew the importance of understanding the text, which was progress. However, when asked to show evidence of their use of a strategy, or to explain how it helped them understand, students too often gave us Kristen's look.

We began to re-examine our teaching. We realized that we had done a great job introducing important comprehension strategies, but had not gone far enough. To use strategies to enhance understanding, our students needed more models, practice, and accountability. As such, we developed studies to introduce, extend, and deepen strategy use to help them become better readers. This book captures that work.

What This Book Contains

In this book, you will find mini-lessons, children's work and words, and a variety of other materials that show our studies in action. Chapter 1 lays the foundation for carrying out studies. We discuss the importance of setting broad literacy goals, defining a daily schedule for reading instruction, and assessing student progress.

The remaining chapters describe strategies we covered in each study. Chapters 2 and 3 address fiction and nonfiction, with ideas for helping students understand the unique structural features of these two genres to successfully navigate texts. Chapters 4 through 8 are devoted to the deep-thinking strategies that research shows good readers use to make meaning: drawing connections, making predictions, getting to know characters, creating mind pictures, and identifying big ideas. Chapter 9 covers book groups, which give students a purpose for applying all strategies simultaneously, pushing them closer to the kind of reading we do as adult readers.

In each strategy chapter, you will find three mini-lessons that demonstrate how to *introduce* the strategy, and *extend* and *deepen* its use. Of course, over the course of a study, you will most likely teach more than three mini-lessons, but these will get you started. (See chart page 6.)

Strategy Study: Making Predictions

Week 1: Introduce Making Predictions

Day 1
- Read Chap. 1 of *Hope's Crossing*.
- Model making realistic predictions.

Day 2
- Read Chap. 2 of *Hope's Crossing*.
- Model making realistic predictions.
- Ask students to make realistic predictions in independent reading.

Day 3
- Read Chap. 3 of *Hope's Crossing*.
- Model making/recording realistic predictions.
- Ask students to make realistic predictions in independent reading.

Day 4
- Read Chap. 4 of *Hope's Crossing*.
- Model making/recording realistic predictions.
- Ask students to record predictions on Prediction/Outcome chart.

Day 5
- Read Chap. 5 of *Hope's Crossing*.
- Model making/recording realistic predictions.
- Ask students to record predictions on Prediction/Outcome chart.

Week 2: Extend Making Predictions

Day 6
- Read Chap. 6 of *Hope's Crossing*.
- Model supporting predictions.
- Ask students to record predictions on Prediction/Outcome chart.

Day 7
- Read Chap. 7 of *Hope's Crossing*.
- Model supporting predictions.
- Ask students to record predictions on Prediction/Outcome chart.

Day 8
- Read Chap. 8 of *Hope's Crossing*.
- Model supporting predictions.
- Ask students to record predictions on Prediction/Outcome chart.

Day 9
- Read Chap. 9 of *Hope's Crossing*.
- Model supporting predictions.
- Ask students to record predictions on Prediction/Outcome chart.

Day 10
- Read Chap. 10 of *Hope's Crossing*.
- Model supporting predictions.
- Ask students to record predictions on Prediction/Outcome chart.

Week 3: Deepen Making Predictions

Day 11
- Read Chap. 11 of *Hope's Crossing*.
- Model updating predictions.
- Ask students to update predictions in independent reading.

Day 12
- Read Chap. 12 of *Hope's Crossing*.
- Model updating predictions.
- Ask students to update predictions in independent reading.

Day 13
- Read Chap. 13 of *Hope's Crossing*.
- Model recording updated predictions.
- Ask students to update predictions in independent reading.

Day 14
- Read Chap. 14 of *Hope's Crossing*.
- Model recording updated predictions.
- Ask students to record updated predictions.

Day 15
- Read Chap. 15 of *Hope's Crossing*.
- Model recording updated predictions.
- Ask students to record updated predictions.

Week 4: Reflect on and Celebrate Making Predictions

Day 16
- Model looking over all recorded predictions.

Day 17
- Model time line and map of predictions.

Day 18
- Invite students to celebrate their work by creating time lines or maps of their own predictions.

Day 19
- Have students work on their time lines and maps.

Day 20
- Allow students to finish their time lines and maps.
- Share.

Each mini-lesson follows a predictable, recursive pattern, similar to the one described in *The Art of Teaching Reading* by Lucy McCormick Calkins (2001). We:

- begin by making a connection between what students already know and what we are going to teach. The connection might relate to an event in the children's lives or to work we've been doing in reading.

- state the purpose of the strategy so what we plan to teach is clear to our students.

- teach what we want students to do. We may teach by modeling, especially when introducing a new strategy. We also teach by reminding students what we want them to think about as we read aloud.

- give students a few minutes to try the strategy and share. We might share as a whole group, in small groups, or in pairs.

- send students off to practice the strategy in independent reading.

- conference with individuals to get a sense of whether they are using the strategy and to what extent.

At the end of each chapter, we include an Assessment and Documentation section with suggestions for gathering students' written responses to books they are reading independently. These responses provide a basis by which to assess and document your students' growth through a strategy study.

Each year, we examine successes and failures. We talk to each other and our colleagues about what is working and what isn't. And we modify our lessons accordingly. So we encourage you to do the same and to use this book in a way that meets your needs. Teach the strategies in any order that you see fit, for example. Do not necessarily follow the mini-lessons to the letter. We hope that you will find our ideas useful and applicable.

Now, we invite you into our classrooms and conversations to see how we teach comprehension strategies to help our students become better readers. Welcome.

◀ *Nicole plans her prediction study. The first three weeks are devoted to guiding students toward using the strategy independently. During the fourth week, students reflect on and celebrate their use of the strategy. See Appendix 1 for a template.*

Creating a Context
for Teaching Comprehension Strategies

Helping children to become life-long readers is the top priority in our classrooms. The ability to read—to understand text of any sort—is essential. On a basic level, reading enables us to do our jobs, participate in our communities, and understand what's happening in the world. On a deeper level, it makes us good thinkers. By teaching children to read well, we teach them to be thoughtful, deliberate problem solvers. We want reading to enrich our students' lives, whether they are doing it for pleasure or out of necessity.

In this chapter, we discuss our basic principles and practices for meeting that goal. We begin by addressing comprehension strategies that good readers use and that form the backbone of our reading curriculum. We then discuss how we structure our day and assess students to move them toward deeper comprehension.

What Good Readers Do

Many recent publications have opened our eyes to the comprehension strategies good readers employ. Good readers:

1. know when they understand what they read. When they don't understand, good readers know how to help themselves.

2. know that some ideas in text are more important than others and can identify those ideas.

3. allow the text to create pictures in their minds' eyes.

4. constantly synthesize new information and existing knowledge as they read.

5. use personal experience and knowledge to make meaning from text.

6. ask questions as they read to gain a better understanding of the text's message.

7. know that often a lot is going on below the surface of a text. Good readers make inferences as they read to form sophisticated understandings.

Moving our students toward life-long reading means helping them use all of these strategies simultaneously and seamlessly. We discuss some of the strategies, such as questioning a text and knowing when you are understanding it, almost every day. Others are taught through more formal studies that last between three and five weeks.

In each study, we *introduce* the strategy by defining and modeling it through read aloud. As the study continues, we *extend* and *deepen* use of the strategy, guiding students toward using it in independent reading. We observe our students, talk to them, listen to them read, and read what they write about reading to get a sense of how they are internalizing the strategies. These studies form the core of this book:

Understanding Elements of Fiction Most stories contain predictable elements such as characters, setting, problem, solution, and a big idea readers take from the text. They may also contain pictures, chapter titles, and other graphic features. When students examine these elements, they begin to think about how these elements might help or hinder their comprehension. This cycle lays the foundation for that kind of strategic work.

Understanding Elements of Nonfiction When we teach our students the unique and varied elements of nonfiction—such as tables of contents, indexes, headings, bold and italic print, photo captions, diagrams, and glossaries—the genre becomes more manageable. These elements help readers navigate text and provide clues about what information is important.

Drawing Connections to Texts Students comprehend best when they can connect what they are reading to their own lives and existing knowledge. So it is

Great Books and Articles on Strategic Reading

Mosaic of Thought
by Ellin Keene and Susan Zimmerman (Heinemann)

Strategies that Work
by Stephanie Harvey and Anne Goudvis (Stenhouse)

Teaching Reading in the Middle School
by Laura Robb (Scholastic)

"Developing Expertise in Reading Comprehension"
by David Pearson et al. (International Reading Association)

The Art of Teaching Reading
by Lucy McCormick Calkins (Longman)

important to help students become cognizant of how reading connects to what they already know. This strategy gives reading a purpose and makes it more pleasurable. It also provides a good context for questioning the text.

Making Predictions Good readers constantly anticipate what will happen next. They make realistic predictions based on what they already know and clues the author provides. Predictions prompt the reader to infer, synthesize, think ahead, and ask questions. As predictions are confirmed, changed, and negated, the reader's engagement in the text increases.

Getting to Know Characters It's important to "step inside" the text and interact with the characters on a personal level. That way, readers come to understand a character's thoughts and actions as they might a real person's. Identifying with a character this way broadens a reader's comprehension of a text.

Creating Mind Pictures When students create a mind picture, they visualize what they are reading. Elements such as setting, character, mood, and details jump off the page and come alive in the imagination. Readers can "see" the author's words, making it easier for them to synthesize text details and their own knowledge and experiences.

Identifying the Big Ideas Most texts contain details and a big idea. Proficient readers are able to distinguish these elements while reading and come away with a clear understanding of the big idea and how the details support it. They can identify the big idea, synthesize information, and draw conclusions for better understanding.

Student-Led Book Groups After studying comprehension strategies, students use them concurrently in book clubs. In groups of two to six, they select the book and decide on a timeframe. They then meet to discuss the book. Book groups allow students to try out strategies in a safe and supportive environment of peers.

You may have already introduced your students to these strategies. If so, consider spending time extending and deepening their use. The following chapters provide you with the necessary tools, regardless of where you are in the process.

Our Daily Routine for Reading Instruction

We teach these strategies during reading workshop, which lasts from one and a half to two hours a day. Topics from social studies, science, and art are integrated through the texts we choose for shared reading, read aloud, and guided reading, as well as by making texts rich in content available for independent reading.

Six Components of Reading Workshop

The following components provide many opportunities each day for us to model the strategies good readers use, for students to discuss and practice them, and for us to assess students' progress.

READ ALOUD (20—25 MINUTES)

Read aloud is at the center of our reading curriculum because it allows students to see strategy use in action. Students can focus on the strategies directly, without having to read the text themselves. Before we begin, we explain how each strategy helps us make meaning. As we read, we model the strategy by thinking aloud about what's going on in our minds. After we read, we ask students to try out the strategy and share their experiences with classmates.

We tend to read longer texts, such as chapter books, that are just above the average reading level of our students. Since these texts cannot be finished in one sitting, they allow us to go beyond simply introducing the strategy, and model more complex and sophisticated ways of using it.

Stephanie reads aloud.

SHARED READING (10—20 MINUTES)

During shared reading, we explore an enlarged piece of text. We might look for words that paint pictures in our minds or passages that reveal a character's personality traits or information about the setting. This close interaction with text is important because it allows students to provide evidence for their thinking. For example, when we ask them, "Why did you make that prediction?" or "How do you know that character likes pancakes?" they can go to the text before them and quote the passage that lead them to their conclusion.

We often find short pieces of text that support our read aloud. For example, if we are reading fiction in read aloud, we might find a related newspaper article or poem for shared reading. This allows us to model comprehension strategies across genres.

INDEPENDENT READING (20—30 MINUTES)

We devote at least twenty minutes each day to independent reading to give students an opportunity to practice all the strategies we've modeled. As reading expert Don Holdaway points out, schools spend most of their time teaching literacy skills, but leave little time for children to practice those skills by actually reading (Braunger and Lewis). Children need to apply strategies to become good at using them.

Stephanie confers with a student during independent reading.

During independent reading, we circulate around the room and conduct conferences with each student at least once a week. We listen to children read, take running records, ask questions about the skills and strategies the child is using, and discuss newly acquired knowledge. We take notes on labels. (See page 14 for more on assessment). In the process, we learn about each child as a reader. We gain evidence of each child's strengths and weaknesses. Often, we follow up on what we taught in a mini-lesson. We check whether students are trying out the strategy on their own and if they're having success.

Our conferences follow a predictable structure. We:

- ask the student what she is reading and the strategies she is working on. Often, we refer to what we discussed in a previous conference to continually move students forward.

- listen to the student read aloud, noting her fluency and use of strategies.

- explore specific places in the text where the student used the strategies she is working on.

- discuss how the student will push herself further. Perhaps the student has been working on one strategy for several weeks and needs to move on. Or she might consistently choose books that are too easy or in the same genre and needs to try something new. We note goals on a label to provide a record of the conference.

Conferences also help us to plan instruction. For example, if we notice only some children struggling with a strategy, we will gather them together in a guided reading group and give them explicit instruction. If we notice that most students are struggling with a specific strategy, we backtrack and address the issue in a whole-class lesson. If we find that only one child is having trouble, we continue one-on-one support. (For more on reading conferences, see page 15.)

GUIDED READING AND READERS RESPOND (30—45 MINUTES)

Guided reading and readers respond take place simultaneously; while we gather a group of students for guided reading, the remainder of the class works on reading responses or continues reading independently.

Guided Reading (10—15 minutes per group) We pull together a group of four to eight students to work on a specific strategy and give each child a copy of a book, article, or poem that we select beforehand.

Nicole meets with a guided reading group.

Nicole's students share what they worked on in reading.

During the meeting, we teach or review a strategy with the expectation that students will begin to employ it in their independent reading. These groups are flexible. They change according to the needs of individual children.

Readers Respond As we meet with guided reading groups, the rest of the class responds to books in writing, using pictures and words, which helps students synthesize what they've read. These responses are also excellent assessment tools because they provide us with evidence of the strategies students are working on. We depend on written responses to see whether students are using the strategies we are teaching and, if so, to what degree.

READERS SHARE (10—20 MINUTES)

Social interaction is crucial in the development of skills and strategies (Braunger and Lewis). Readers share allows students to share orally what they've been working on, with the whole class or in small groups. They talk about strategies, new knowledge, successes, and failures. They learn from and help one another. They develop their capacities to reflect, since they must think deeply about their reading in order to describe it to others. Readers share is also a powerful assessment and accountability tool because we hear about reading experiences directly from the students.

Assessing Student Progress

Gathering Data

When we assess our students in reading, we take the stance of researchers. We observe students, listen carefully, and use resources and tools to gather a wealth of valuable information. We also ask thoughtful questions, such as:

- What type of reader is this student?
- What can I do for this student as a reader?
- What strategy does the student already use?
- What reading strategy do I need to teach this student next?

Formal and informal assessments help us to understand our students completely. For example, we keep running records to gather information on each student's reading level, the types of errors and self-corrections he makes, and whether his book choices are appropriate. We take records based on self-selected books and benchmark books (i.e. books that reflect an average reading level at a particular grade).

Reading conferences are a valuable type of informal assessment. They help us stay abreast of students' book choices, evaluate their comprehension, and determine the reading strategies they're employing. We conduct a reading conference with each student at least once a week, recording information we gather on a label. (See example right.) Labels provide enough space to jot down information; a sheet of them fits conveniently on a clipboard.

By the end of the week, it's easy to distinguish the students we've conferred with and those we haven't. After filling a sheet of labels, we affix labels to each student's page in our assessment binder, which gives us an ongoing picture of the child's growth as a reader. (See example on page 16.) We get a sense of whether the student is taking risks in reading or sticking to what he already knows.

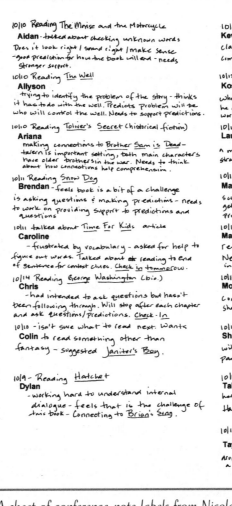

10/10 Reading The Mouse and the Motorcycle
Aidan - talked about checking unknown words
Does it look right / sound right / make sense
- good prediction for how the book will end - needs
stronger support

10/10 Reading The Well
Allyson
- trying to identify the problem of the story - thinks
it has to do with the well. Predicts problem will be
who will control the well. Needs to support predictions.

10/10 Reading Toliver's Secret (historical fiction)
Ariana
making connections to Brother Sam is Dead -
tavern is important setting, both main characters
have older brothers in the war. Needs to think
about how connections help comprehension.

10/11 Reading Snow Dog
Brendan - feels book is a bit of a challenge
is asking questions & making predictions - needs
to work on providing support to predictions and
questions

10/11 talked about Time For Kids article
Caroline
- frustrated by vocabulary - asked for help to
figure out words. Talked about reading to end
of sentence for context clues. Check in tommorow.

10/14 Reading George Washington (bio.)
Chris
- had intended to ask questions but hasn't
been following through. Will stop after each chapter
and ask questions/predictions. Check-In

10/10 - isn't sure what to read next. Wants
Colin to read something other than
fantasy - suggested Janitor's Boy.

10/9 - Reading Hatchet
Dylan
- working hard to understand internal
dialogue - feels that is the challenge of
this book - Connecting to Brian's Song.

10/13
Kevin - wants to try out Downsiders - so many
classmates have enjoyed it. Will test it - check
comprehension after the first chapter, then decide.

10/12 Joey Pigza Swallows the Key
Kostas - predicted that something bad would happen
when Joey was playing with the scissors - Outcome -
he cut off the tip of Maria's nose - Needs to
work on stronger support

10/11 - Harry Potter # 3
Lauren - talked about how she relies on "making
a movie in her head." Will work on other
strategies like connections & predictions.

10/14 - Joey Pigza
Matt - made prediction that Joey will go to the
school for kids with disabilities because he's
getting tested. Check in tomorrow to see if
prediction has an instance

10/15 Island of the Amerts
Mackenzie - very expressive reading - good
re-telling of what has happened so far.
Needs to work on articulating what's going on
in her head while she reads.

10/14 Hitler Stole the Pink Rabbit
Morgan - just started it. Thinks making
connections will be a helpful strategy b/c
she's read so many books about the Holocaust

10/12 - Time for Kids
Shayra - talked about checking comprehension
with non-fiction by trying to say the
paragraph in own words - Will try it Check
In

10/16 - Harry Potter #3
Tabitha - thinks making predictions focuses
her reading - reading on for specific reason.
Has great support for her predictions.

10/12 - Torn Thread
Taylor - making predictions but frustrated b/c
something he thinks is important sometimes
drops right out of the book. Talked about how that's
a good time to update predictions.

A sheet of conference-note labels from Nicole's clipboard.

These reading conference notes give a clear picture of Caroline's strengths and weaknesses.

9.4
Caroline - goal is to expand her reading. Reads primarily fantasy.
Can find word meanings from context clues in fiction.

9.5 Reading The Smugglers
Caroline - choose b/c she read The Wreckers same author. Can re-tell the story. Not yet sharing her feelings toward the book.

9.11 Reading Downsiders
Caroline - can re-tell the story - not enjoying it. Can't decide btw Smugglers & Downsiders. Convinced her to stick with Smuggles - higher interest.

10/03 House at Pooh Corner
Caroline - asking "I wonder" questions as she reads. Talked about how it's okay to have questions that are not answered.

10/11 - House at Pooh Corner
Caroline - Reading journal shows lots of re-telling of stories and some connections. Needs to focus on how connections help comprehension.

10/17 - Reading Poppy
Caroline - asking great questions and making great predictions. Needs to work on stronger support for questions & predictions.

10/11 - talked about Time for Kids article.
Caroline - frustrated by vocabulary - asked for help to figure out words. Talked about reading to end of sentence for context clues. Check in tomorrow.

10/13 - Reading article on Revolutionary War Weapons.
Caroline - replaced unknown word (artillery) with a word that would make sense (weapons). Feels better about unknown vocab. in nonfiction.

In addition to conferences, students' written responses inform us of the extent to which they are comprehending. They help us to see the reading strategies students are using and those they aren't. Written responses are excellent self-reflection tools as well, because they enhance students' understanding of what they've read and clarify questions for them.

Organizing Assessments to Inform Our Teaching

Finding a system to organize assessments is extremely beneficial to planning instruction and communicating with administrators and parents. We keep the students' assessments in binders, which contain a section for each student. Each section contains running records and information from conferences.

We also devote a section of the binder to "whole-class needs." In it, among other kinds of notes, are sheets of reading conference labels, which we photocopy prior to putting individual labels into individual student sections. This enables us to look for patterns of needs and to teach to those needs. For example, upon reviewing a week's worth of labels, Stephanie can tell that:

- Sergio, Winnie, and Katrina all are reading books from the same series. She may want to introduce book clubs to them.

- Jayvon and Marilyn are struggling with making connections to their books. They are applying only letter-sound correspondence as they read, which may signal an inappropriate book choice. Stephanie may want to pull the students together in a guided reading group to investigate this further and take a running record to check their levels.

- Sherrie is rereading a lot of books and not challenging herself. Stephanie supports Sherrie by directing her to a slightly higher level of series books with predictable text structures and characters. She will check in with Sherrie throughout the week.

In addition to our assessments, students maintain a portfolio of work. The portfolio shows the student's progress from the beginning of the year to the end. With our input, students select pieces that demonstrate their growth most strongly. They take their portfolio home at different points in the year to share with parents.

Assessments help us gather the information we need to teach our students to read strategically, which makes moving students toward life-long reading a reality.

Closing Thoughts

It is important to set clear teaching goals, create daily routines that help you meet those goals, and determine whether you're meeting goals by assessing students regularly. In essence, create the framework of a successful year of literacy instruction. Once the framework is in place, the teaching begins. The rest of this book describes cycles of study for introducing, extending, and deepening students' reading comprehension.

Understanding Elements of Fiction

In a recent conference about *The Phantom Tollbooth*, Matt questioned whether the main character, Milo, would make it home. After thinking about it, he concluded, "Of course he will. This is a kid's book. They *always* end happily." We teach students to use what they know about fiction as a way to check their comprehension. If a student cannot identify the predictable elements of fiction, such as characters, setting, problem, solution, and author's overall message, chances are he or she is not comprehending and needs to apply strategies. That's what this chapter is all about.

We suggest studying the elements of fiction early in the year because it will be useful in learning strategies that you teach later. Students will be able to make connections to characters and setting more easily. They will predict how the story's problem will be solved. They will look for the story's big idea by thinking about the author's message.

OVERVIEW
of the Study

Over the course of our four-week study, we:

- ۞ introduce the elements of fiction by brainstorming what we know about it.

- ۞ extend students' knowledge by asking them to identify the elements of fiction in small groups.

- ۞ deepen their understanding by asking them to use elements of fiction to check their comprehension.

We constantly watch students and listen to their questions, looking for mini-lesson topics. The lessons that follow represent a few we might teach. Throughout the study, we continually assess students formally and informally, taking notes as we conference with individuals and observe partners at work. To document their learning, we ask students to complete story maps, which we describe on page 25.

Choosing Read-Aloud Texts to Teach Elements of Fiction

To teach students to identify the elements of fiction, you need a collection of stories that they can read in small groups, without your support. The stories should also have a similar plot line. The many versions of *Cinderella* are excellent for younger children because the story remains the same. Only the details change from book to book. Reading stories with similar plot lines reinforces the fact that all fiction shares many of the same basic elements.

With older, more proficient readers, you might use an anthology such as *A Treasury of Dragon Stories*. With less proficient readers, stories from the *Little Bear* or *Lionel series* work well because they contain discrete stories with predictable characters, settings, and text structures.

Cinderella Stories

The Egyptian Cinderella
by Shirley Climo
(HarperCollins)

The Irish Cinderlad
by Shirley Climo
(HarperCollins)

Yeh-Shen
by Ai-Ling Louie
(Philomel)

The Rough-Faced Girl
by Rafe Martin
(Putnam)

Cinderella
by Charles Perrault
(Knopf)

Cendrillon
by Daniel San Souci
(Simon and Schuster)

Mufaro's Beautiful Daughters
by John Steptoe
(Lothrop, Lee, and Shepard)

Introduce the Strategy

Brainstorming What We Know About Fiction

Purpose

To create a common vocabulary for studying the elements of fiction. To give you an idea of how much students already know about how fiction works.

Materials and Preparation

A collection of stories that contain similar characters, settings, and/or text structures, such as the Cinderella stories. Chart paper to list students' ideas.

1. DISCUSS WHAT STUDENTS KNOW

Nicole gathers all students and displays the *Cinderella* stories.

Nicole: Who knows the story of Cinderella?

(Most hands shoot up.)

Nicole: If I were to read this story, what would I find? *(Charts the students' responses: "a prince, evil stepmother, evil stepsisters, fairy godmother, Cinderella, a castle, a ball, and magic")* Great! These are the things we would expect to find in *Cinderella*. How can we categorize these elements?

Mackenzie: You could put prince, evil stepmother, Cinderella, evil stepsisters, and fairy godmother together because they're people.

Nicole: Great job, Mackenzie. Does anyone know the word we use to describe the people in books?

Tabitha: Characters?

Nicole: That's right. Stories contain characters. What do we call where the story takes place, like at the ball in the castle?

Kevin: Setting?

Nicole: Great. Will we find these things only in this book, *Cinderella*?

(Students shake their heads.)

Nicole: That's right. We know all fictional stories have characters and a setting. We also know that something happens in a story. There is a problem and the problem is solved. What is the problem in *Cinderella*?

Shayra: Cinderella is treated really badly by her stepmother and stepsisters. They make her do all the work around the house.

Nicole: That's the problem. How is it solved?

Shayra: A fairy godmother helps her go to a ball and meet a prince who takes her away from her evil stepmother.

Nicole: That's the solution to the problem. Cinderella gets away from her wicked stepmother with some help from her fairy godmother and a prince.

2. READ ALOUD

Nicole: Now let's read this French version of the Cinderella story and see if we find the characters, setting, problem, and solution we expect. *(Reads aloud the Charles Perrault version of Cinderella, the "Disney" version.)* Was there anything unexpected in the story?

(Students shrug. Some say, "Not really.")

Nicole: There is one more element of fiction that we haven't talked about. Writers convey a message. What do you think the author's message is in this *Cinderella? (Pauses.)* I think it might be that being a good person is always better than being a mean one, because Cinderella, the good character, got what she wanted and her stepmother and stepsisters did not.

Colin: Yeah, good conquers evil!

3. CHART OBSERVATIONS

With the class, Nicole creates a list of the elements of fiction, which students refer to throughout the study. (See sample below.)

FOLLOW-UP

In reading conferences, ask students to identify the characters, setting, problem, solution, and author's message of their self-selected books. Expect students to use those words when talking about books.

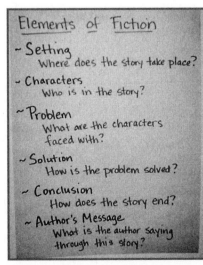

A chart of elements of fiction that the class created.

Do you understand the work of fiction you are reading?

Use this checklist to make sure you comprehend the basics of the story.

- ☺ *Who are the main characters?*

- ☺ *Where does the story take place?*

- ☺ *What is the main problem in the story?*

- ☺ *How is the problem solved?*

- ☺ *How does the story end?*

- ☺ *What message is the author trying to tell you through the story?*

Photocopy this bookmark and distribute it to students.

Extend the Strategy
Identifying Elements of Fiction

Purpose

To help students identify elements of fiction independently, in pairs

Materials and Preparation

A collection of stories that contain similar characters, settings, and/or text structures, such as the Cinderella stories. Chart paper to list students' ideas.

1. INTRODUCE THE LESSON

Nicole gathers all students and displays the Cinderella stories and "Elements of Fiction" chart.

Nicole: Yesterday we read *Cinderella*. We identified the characters, setting, problem, and solution and began to talk about the author's message. Today, you are going to read another version of Cinderella with a partner. As you read, identify the elements of fiction as we did yesterday. *Points to "Elements of Fiction" chart.* This list we made yesterday will be right here for you to refer to.

2. PAIR UP STUDENTS

Nicole asks students to read in pairs and help each other identify basic elements, making sure that each student reads a version of the story at an appropriate reading level. She knows this is a logical step between whole-class and independent learning.

3. SHARE AS A WHOLE GROUP

After giving partners adequate time to read, Nicole invites them back to the meeting area.

Nicole: What did you find?

Tatiana: I was reading *Yeh-Shen* with Adaly. The elements were pretty much the same as in *Cinderella*. Yeh-Shen was treated really badly by her stepmother. There wasn't a fairy godmother, but there was a magical fish that helped her.

Nicole: What about the setting?

Tatiana: The story takes place at Yeh-Shen's house and then at the palace of a rich man.

Nicole: So the setting was the same too?

Tatiana: It was sort of the same but the pictures were really different.

Nicole: Why do you think the pictures are different?

Tatiana: Because the story is from China so the pictures are of people and houses there.

FOLLOW-UP

After students have read the stories and talked about them, have them record elements, with examples from the books, on chart paper. These charts will make it easier for students to compare all the stories. They will also allow you to assess whether they are able to identify the elements of fiction.

MINI-LESSON

Deepen the Strategy
Using Elements of Fiction

1. INTRODUCE THE LESSON

Nicole's class has identified elements of fiction as a whole group and in partners. Now she wants them to use what they've learned to help check their comprehension. She begins by gathering the students together.

Nicole: We've learned that all fiction has several predictable elements: characters, setting, a problem, a solution, and a message the author is trying to convey to the reader. Now that we know that these elements are always present in a work of fiction, we can use them to see if we are understanding what we read. I've made a "Checklist of Fictional Elements" we can use during read aloud. *(Points to chart.)* And I've made bookmark checklists for you to use when you read independently.

2. MODEL THE STRATEGY

Nicole: I'm going to read one of my favorite stories, *Alligator Baby* by Robert Munsch. As I read, I'm going to make sure I can identify the elements of fiction. If I can't identify an element, what do you think I should do?

Taylor: Re-read?

Purpose

To show students how to monitor comprehension, using a checklist of fictional elements

Materials and Preparation

Pre-read a picture book to read to your class. Prepare a "Checklist of Fictional Elements" chart and photocopy a smaller, bookmark version for each student. (See pages 21 and 24.)

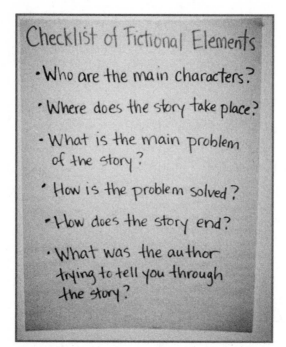

Nicole charts a checklist of fictional elements and models how to use it independently.

Nicole: Absolutely. If I don't know the characters, setting, or another element, I will re-read. In order to comprehend a story, I need to be able to identify the elements of fiction. *(Begins to read* Alligator Baby. *After the first few pages she pauses.)* I've come to a break in the text so I'll stop here and check my comprehension. Who are the main characters? Well, there's the boy, his mother, and his father. I don't know their names. I'll flip back through the book and see if their names have been introduced. *(Flips through the pages she's read.)* No, the author has not told me their names. What about the setting? This story takes place in this family's home and at the zoo. The problem is that the parents keep bringing home baby animals from the hospital, not their own human baby. I don't know how the problem will be solved yet, so I'll continue reading. *(Continues to read, stopping every few pages to see if she has more information about the elements of fiction. At the end of the story, she identifies the solution and the author's message.)*

Nicole: Now it's your turn. As you read independently today, identify the elements of fiction to make sure you understand. You can use these bookmarks as a reminder. *(Gives a bookmark to each student before they go off to read.)*

3. CONFER WITH INDIVIDUAL STUDENTS

Nicole noticed that Shayra didn't share much during the mini-lessons, so she sits down with her for a conference.

Nicole: Hi, Shayra. How's your reading going today?

Shayra: Great! I'm reading the second *The Secrets of Droon: Journey to the Volcano Palace.*

Nicole: Do you understand what you read?

Shayra: Yup, I'm using my bookmark to help me remember what I need to check for.

Nicole: Can you tell me a little bit about how you're checking your comprehension?

Shayra:	Well, after the first chapter, I stopped and asked myself, "Who are the main characters?"—just like you did during read aloud.
Nicole:	Who are the main characters?
Shayra:	*(Closes the book.)* These two kids on the cover.
Nicole:	What are their names?
Shayra:	Shoot! I forgot. I knew a few seconds ago.
Nicole:	What are you going to do?
Shayra:	I guess I should re-read and find out their names.
Nicole:	Excellent. You are using the checklist! Keep up the great work!

Conferences like this will give you a lot of information about how well your students can identify the elements of fiction in their independent reading. Here are some questions we typically ask:

- ◉ Who are the main characters?
- ◉ Which are the good characters and which are evil?
- ◉ Where does this story take place?
- ◉ What is the big problem facing the main character in the story?

Assessment and Documentation

Conference notes provide excellent informal assessment information. Also, listen to the thoughts students share in mini-lessons, readers share, and guided reading. Do students know how to find out who a character is, where the story takes place, and what the central problem is? Be sure to continue working with those who struggle.

To assess students more formally, ask them to complete a story map when they've finished a story. (See sample on page 26.) Or have them complete one as they read, stopping every now and then to add information. You can customize maps so they ask students to identify specific elements about the story or the genre. (See Appendix 2 for a story map template.)

Teacher Tip

Guided reading provides an excellent starting point to get students in the habit of identifying the basic elements of a story. You can introduce a story, have students read the first few pages, discuss the characters, setting, and problem, and then allow students to finish the story independently.

Name: Winnie   Date: 2/16

Story Map

Title: The Chalk Box Kid   Author: Bulla

Characters: Gregory, Ivy, Richard, Miss perry, Vance
Uncle Max

Setting: The setting took Place in his home and in his
school and at the turned building.

Problem: Gregory problem was he made a garden out of
chalk and he told the Kids that he had a garden

Solution: Gregory solved it by the teacher telling Gregory
can she come to his house and Miss. Perry looked
at the garden and said it was beautiful.

Conclusion: In the last part all his friends were
friendly to him. And his uncle Max put back his
picture on the walls.

Author's Message: _____
_____
_____
_____

On the back of this story map, draw the most important part of the story.

Winnie's story map of THE
CHALK BOX KID by Clyde Bulla.

Closing Thoughts

We find that most students learn to use the elements of fiction to check comprehension rather easily. But there are always some who need additional instruction. When the majority of your students can identify elements of fiction in their reading, it's time to move on to another study. We usually follow the fiction study with a nonfiction study, so that students get a clear understanding of the differences between the two genres.

CHAPTER 3

Understanding Elements of Nonfiction

We come in contact with nonfiction every day: maps, menus, guides, brochures, newspapers, magazines, and the Internet. Therefore, studying it has real-life value for students. However, the elements of nonfiction, such as tables of contents, indexes, headings, bold and italic print, photo captions, diagrams, and glossaries, are different from those of fiction. When students are aware of how nonfiction works, they are more apt to comprehend it. Specifically, they can tackle various kinds of nonfiction, navigate the text, and distinguish important ideas from less important ones.

We suggest studying the elements of nonfiction early in the year for the same reason we suggested studying the elements of fiction: because it will be useful in learning strategies that you teach later. Students will use what they know about nonfiction, for example, to make predictions. They will use nonfiction knowledge to think about the book's big idea. And they will use it while tackling their own independent inquiries.

OVERVIEW
of the Study

Over the course of our four-week study, we:

- introduce students to the structure and layout of nonfiction.

- extend their understanding of those elements.

- deepen understanding by using elements to find information.

Making this happen requires time and support. During the study, we immerse students in nonfiction. For the first few days, we read aloud from a variety of nonfiction books so that students become familiar with content, organization, and tone. We allow students to practice strategies during shared reading and support their growth through guided, paired, and independent reading of non-fiction. We also conduct mini-lessons on navigating nonfiction. The lessons described in this chapter only represent a few. We plan and tailor lessons based on students' needs.

Choosing Read-Aloud Texts to Teach Elements of Nonfiction

It is important to be selective. We look for books that are well written, are simple in structure and organization, and contain clear ideas supported by strong details.

Making students aware of the different kinds of nonfiction is important, too. Sometimes we use traditional information books; other times we use narrative nonfiction, which may look like picture or chapter books, but the information they hold is factual. For instance, we might read *China* from the Postcards series because of its useful table of contents, glossary, and index. Then we might read a narrative nonfiction book, such as *Chasing the Moon to China*, to show how, even though its layout and tone are different, we can still extract information from it. Then we might share *Amazing Snakes*, an Eyewitness Juniors book, because of its clear headings, *Taking Your Camera To . . .* series because of its clear captions and photographs, and *From Cow to Milk Carton* because of its easy-to-follow layout. Finally, we might share *Koko's Story* by Dr. Francine Patterson or books by Gail Gibbons, such as *Apples*, because of their pleasing, narrative voice.

MINI-LESSON

Introduce the Strategy
Noticing Structure and Layout

1. INTRODUCE THE LESSON

Stephanie gathers her students and displays the nonfiction books they have read.

Stephanie: This week we have been reading a lot of different types of nonfiction. We read *Apples*, *From Cow to Milk Carton*, *Taking Your Camera To France*, *Koko's Story*, and *Postcards from China*. *(Points to the books displayed.)* What are you noticing about nonfiction?

Colleen: The books are all true, and they are about different topics.

Grant: I know that nonfiction books are true, but some seem like picture books.

Stephanie: Exactly. Nonfiction books are factual, but they can vary in what they look like—their layout—and their topics.

2. DISCUSS WHAT STUDENTS NOTICE

Stephanie: Today, we are going to look at the pages of several books and talk about what we are noticing about their layout. *(Holds up* Postcards

Purpose

To explore the structure and layout of non-fiction books

Materials and Preparation

A collection of nonfiction texts on different topics and with different layouts. Chart paper to keep track of what students notice.

Teacher Tip

*Reinforce elements
of nonfiction
during reading
workshop:*

◎ *Use guided
reading to meet
with students
who struggle
to identify
elements.*

◎ *Meet with
students during
reading confer-
ences to direct
them to
just-right
books.*

◎ *During shared
reading, model
how to move
between text,
captions, and
pictures; how
to connect text
and visuals;
and how
to tackle
books with
and without
headings.*

from China *and shows the class a page.)* When I look at this book, I notice that it has a photo with a caption on one page, and a letter on the other page. I am also noticing that there are words that are darker than the others. This is called bold.

Harry: I noticed that there is a table of contents, too.

Stephanie: Right! So far, we have noticed that this book's layout has a table of contents, captions, bold type, and letters. *(Flips through* Apples *with the students.)*

Emily: I remember this book. It has all drawings! It looks like a picture book.

Stephanie: Yes, nonfiction sometimes looks like picture books in the way the words and art are arranged on the page.

Grant: This book is written in paragraphs, too, kind of like *Koko's Story.* But *Koko's Story* has photos. It also felt like a story when we read it.

Stephanie: You are both right. These books are told like a story, and arranged like a picture book, but we learn facts by reading them. *(Picks up* Taking Your Camera to France.*)* Now this book has a table of contents, and its pages are arranged by topic. On every page there are headings, photos, captions, and bold words. Do you notice how sometimes a photo is placed right in the middle of words so that the words go around the photo?

Harry: That's a lot of things on one page. That is confusing sometimes.

Stephanie: You are right. The layout of the page, and elements like captions, bold words, graphs, and arrows, can affect our reading.

FOLLOW-UP

For several days during reading workshop, students work in pairs, looking at and reading a variety of nonfiction books. They keep track of the books' topics and what they notice about their structures and layouts.

At the end of each workshop, Stephanie gathers the students to share what they are noticing, which is usually a lot. Some texts are presented in random chunks and others in straight columns. Some are written in a narrative format and others in a more traditional expository format. Some are broken into sections like chapter books. Some have captions. Stephanie and her students make a list of these different structures.

Extend the Strategy
Using Elements of Nonfiction

1. DISCUSS WHAT STUDENTS KNOW

Stephanie: We have noticed that there are certain elements in a lot of nonfiction texts. For example, there is a table of contents.

Grant: Some have indexes and glossaries.

Ellie: I found books with bold and italic print.

Harry: That book we read about a cow had diagrams and maps.

Emily: *Postcards from China* had photos and captions.

Stephanie: Good. *(Makes a list of the elements of nonfiction to refer to throughout the study. [See sample below.])* These elements of nonfiction help us make sense of what we are reading.

Features of a Nonfiction Text
- captions
- maps
- keys
- bold words & words in italic
- headings
- charts
- diagrams
- labels
- arrows pointing at information
- glossary
- index
- table of contents
- photographs & pictures

Stephanie creates a chart for use throughout her study of nonfiction.

Purpose

To help students use elements independently as tools for constructing meaning

Materials and Preparation

A nonfiction text that your students know and has common elements such as a table of contents, index, headings, bold and italic print, glossary, photo captions, diagrams, and maps. Make a transparency of a representative two-page spread. We used From Cow to Milk Carton, *pages 4 and 5.*

2. EXPLORE A TEXT CLOSELY

Stephanie: Today, we are going to explore how to use these elements. Let's revisit the book *From Cow to Milk Carton*. *(Shows the class the book and pages 4 and 5 on the overhead, which have a heading, running text, and a diagram of a cow's four stomachs, illustrating how food travels through the animal.)*

Stephanie: What are you noticing about this page of text?

Sarah: The page has a heading called *The Body Machine*, and there are paragraphs.

Paul: There is a diagram of a cow and its stomach has numbers on it.

McKenzie: There is another diagram, but I am not sure what it means.

Stephanie: There is a heading, paragraphs, and diagrams. Let's start with the heading. How can it help us as readers?

Sarah: It is like a title. I think it is telling us what the page is about. But that is a weird title. I don't really know what we are going to read.

Stephanie: Right. Let's read a few paragraphs and see if they help us understand the heading. *(Reads aloud. From paragraph one, the class learns that a cow spends most of her time eating, and swallows grass without chewing. In paragraph two, the class learns that a cow uses four stomachs to digest food.)*

Harry: That is so cool! I wish I could swallow my food and have four stomachs to digest it.

Tasia: Yeah, but your stomach only turns it into cud and then you'd have to bring it back up and chew it up.

Stephanie: Wow, you have learned a lot. Harry, how did you know there are four stomachs?

Harry: We read it, but I thought I read wrong. So I looked at the diagram, and there is a drawing of four stomachs labeled.

Stephanie: I am so glad you are using the diagrams and labels to help you make sense of what you are reading. That is what good readers do. *(Points to the diagram entitled "grass.")* Tasia, do you know which stomachs turn the grass into cud?

Tasia: I can't remember. I looked at the diagram. It has the stomach numbers and arrows, but I can't figure it out.

Stephanie: This diagram doesn't tell you every detail. The diagram and the arrows only tell you the path the food travels. Most diagrams work best if you understand the writing, too. To get the most information from this diagram, you have to understand the paragraphs above it. So, let's reread. *(Continues exploring how to use elements to make sense of information.)*

FOLLOW-UP

Over the next few days, Stephanie models how to use nonfiction elements with a variety of nonfiction books. In shared reading and guided reading, she works on using tables of contents, indexes, headings, bold and italic print, glossaries, photo captions, diagrams, and maps, making sure that students are using these elements to build comprehension. Students also continue to read nonfiction in pairs and independently.

MINI-LESSON

Deepen the Strategy
Reading for Specific Information

1. DISCUSS WHAT STUDENTS KNOW

Stephanie: Today we are going to learn how the elements of text can help us when we are searching for specific information. You expressed interest in learning more about how Nigerians celebrate Ramadan and Id-ul-Fitr. So, I found two books on Africa, *Food and Festivals: West Africa* and *A Is for Africa.* How can we tell if the book will give us the information we want?

McKenzie: We could flip through it and look at the pictures.

Stephanie: Let's give that a try.

2. EXPLORE A TEXT CLOSELY

Stephanie shows *A Is for Africa's* cover and flips through the text with the students.

Stephanie: I notice there are headings and lots of pictures, but no captions, table

Purpose

To teach students to search for information purposefully—to use the elements of nonfiction to find information they seek

Materials and Preparation

Two nonfiction books on similar subjects. Make two transparencies of a representative page from each book. We used Food and Festivals: West Africa *and* A Is for Africa, *pages 12 and 13.*

Teacher Tip

During reading conferences about nonfiction, try these questions:

- ◎ *What topic are you reading about?*

- ◎ *How is your book organized?*

- ◎ *What elements are helping you make sense of your reading?*

- ◎ *Is there anything about the structure or layout that is confusing or that you noticed?*

- ◎ *Has your reading sparked any questions that you want to learn more about?*

- ◎ *How are you going to go about finding the answers to your questions?*

of contents, or index. It might take us a while to find the information we need. Let's look at the other book. *(Shows* Food and Festivals: West Africa's *cover and flips through the text.)*

Harry: This book has a table of contents!

Stephanie: This book's layout is clear. It has elements that will help us find information quickly. Lets' take a look at the table of contents to see if there's any information on Ramadan or Id-ul-Fitr. *(Turns to the table of contents, holds up the book, and reads the chapter titles aloud.)*

Emily: We can find out about celebrations and Ramadan on page 12.

Stephanie: *(Turns on the overhead and projects the page.)* What elements on this page might help us make sense of what we are reading?

Grant: It has a heading that says "Ramadan." That tells us what the page is about. It also has photos and captions. I bet those give us more information, too.

Stephanie and the class read on and determine that the page also has a boxed insert, diagrams, and running text about Ramadan. They use these elements to gather information. They also turn to the index to determine whether it, too, will help them find information they need.

FOLLOW-UP

Stephanie asks students to choose a topic, choose books on that topic, and work with partners to find information they are curious about. Working with partners is a good transition between modeling reading and reading independently.

Assessment and Documentation

To assess student's understanding of nonfiction elements, listen to their thoughts in readers share, guided reading, and conferences.

- ◎ Do students know how to use a table of contents, an index, and a glossary?

- ◎ Can they move easily between those elements and running text?

- ◎ Does their reading raise questions, and can they find answers in books?

- ◎ Continue to work with those students who struggle in guided reading and during reading conferences.

To assess students more formally, ask them to fill out a nonfiction response

Student Stephanie completes a nonfiction response sheet.

Paul writes up what he learned from reading BASEBALL'S SLUGGERS AND PITCHERS.

baseball's Sluggers and Pitchers 11-15
Paul

Sammy Sosa was born 11-12-01.
Three days ago. Derek Jeter
owns the record for most runs
scored by a shortstop (352).
Curt Schilling had his
birthday yesterday 11-14-01.
barry bonds together with
his Dad Bobby. he holds the
all-time major league record
for home runs by a father
and son. They have more then
750 homers between them!
Pedro Martinez was the winning
Pitcher and MVP of the
1999 All-Star game. Ken Griffey
Junior's birthday is in 6
Days. 11-21-01. As a boy
Roger Clemens loved the
yankees. in 1999, he joined
his Dream team! Mo Vaughn's
birthday is 2 days away
from Mine. 12-15-01 Mine is
12-17-01. Mike Piazza has hit more than

an 300 career homeruns.
I like the book! because
It's about baseball. I did not
no eny of these things!

sheet when they finish a book. (See sample above and Appendix 3.) Also, have them write in journals about what they learned from their reading. (See sample right.)

Closing Thoughts

The amount of time you put into studying the elements of nonfiction depends on the needs of your students. Because this was the students' introduction to nonfiction elements, Stephanie conducted many lessons and discussions. Care was taken to choose clear models that students could comprehend. Time was given for students to practice using the elements to make sense of their reading. Although we moved on to a new study, our conversations about nonfiction continued throughout the year, as students grew as readers.

Drawing Connections to Texts

Reading is a little like rock climbing. A climber needs to find footholds in a sheer rock face to reach the top of it. A reader needs to find footholds in a text to comprehend it. Connections are a reader's footholds. As she reads, she builds comprehension by connecting what she knows to what's in the text. Connections give her something familiar to grab onto.

When making connections, a student might think, "Wow, this reminds me of my life" or "This is just like a story I read last week," going beyond a literal interpretation of the text. These moments of recognition can lead to complex questions that enhance understanding. For example, while reading *Freckle Juice* by Judy Blume, Eryka explains, "Andrew is making this concoction of stuff that Sharon said would give him freckles. My cousin and I did that once. We mixed together all kinds of stuff that we found in the fridge. We got so sick. I wonder if Andrew is going to get sick from drinking that stuff." By making a connection to her life, Eryka asks an informed question of the text. As she reads, she'll look for the answer. Reading in this purposeful way will cause Eryka to read more deeply.

OVERVIEW
of the Study

We teach drawing connections in three phases, over four weeks. Specifically, we:

- ✹ introduce the strategy, teaching students to look for relationships between their experiences and the text.

- ✹ extend the strategy, teaching students to look for relationships between what they are currently reading and what they have read in the past.

- ✹ deepen the strategy, teaching students to use connections to ask realistic, informed questions that lead to richer understanding.

By carrying our mini-lessons on all of these topics, we show children how to use their experience and knowledge to make meaning from text. Our goal is not only to get students to use the strategy, but to articulate how it helps their comprehension.

Great Books to Model Drawing Connections

The Pain and the Great One
by Judy Blume
(Bradbury Press)

Nasty Sticky Sneakers
by Eve Bunting
(HarperCollins)

Because of Winn Dixie
by Kate Dicamillo
(Candlewick Press)

The Classroom at the End of the Hall
by Douglas Evan
(Scholastic)

The War with Grandpa
by Robert Kimmell Smith (Delacorte)

Choosing a Read-Aloud Text to Teach Drawing Connections

For this study, you should find a read aloud your students can connect to on a personal level. The characters may come from backgrounds similar to those of your students. The setting may resemble a place with which they are familiar. What's most important is that you find a book that your class will relate to.

We chose *The Stories Julian Tells* by Ann Cameron because the main character is our students' age and shares their humor, interests, and experiences. It is made up of six short stories about Julian and his younger brother, Huey. Julian is always telling stories, dreaming, and getting into mischief. Ann Cameron's powerful language enables readers to identify with the way Julian feels when he eats all the pudding his father made for his mother, to feel his shame about convincing Huey that catalogs contain real cats that work in a garden, and to understand his childish belief that eating the leaves off a fig tree will help him grow. Julian is, indeed, a lovable character to which many 7- to 9-year-olds can relate.

Introduce the Strategy
Making Personal Connections

Purpose

To show students that good readers connect what they read to their own experiences to enhance reading

Materials and Preparation

Choose a read-aloud text and identify a connection you can make between the story and your own life.

1. INTRODUCE THE LESSON

Nicole begins this lesson by identifying personal connections as a strategy good readers use to make meaning as they read.

Nicole: We are going to begin a new read aloud today, *The Stories Julian Tells* by Ann Cameron. I chose this book because when I read it, it reminded me so much of my own childhood. Has that ever happened to you, you read a book or see something in a movie or on television and you think, "Wow, that really reminds me of something that happened in my life?" That happens to me all the time.

Kosta: When I was reading *Baseball Fever* I kept thinking that the kid in the story is just like me because he loves sports and I love sports.

2. STATE THE PURPOSE OF THE STRATEGY

Nicole: Kosta, you did something that good readers do. You connected what you were reading to your own life. That's what we're going to begin studying today, making connections to what we read. As I read *The Stories Julian Tells*, I will share the connections I make between this book and my own life. I want you to think about how you can connect this book to your lives because we will also share your connections.

3. MODEL THE STRATEGY

Nicole reads the first six pages aloud. In the story, Julian and Huey's father makes lemon pudding and tells the boys that the pudding is for their mother and they shouldn't touch it. Nicole pauses to share her connection.

Nicole: This reminds me so much of when I was little and I would sit in the kitchen and watch my grandfather make cakes. The kitchen would get hot and my grandfather's arms seemed to be able to do a million things just like Julian's father. *(Continues reading, stopping every few pages to share personal connections.)*

4. SHARE AS A WHOLE GROUP

After sharing her own connections, Nicole encourages her students to try out the strategy.

Nicole: I shared some connections I made to this text. Did any of you make connections as I was reading?

Tatiana: When you read the part about how Julian's father was squeezing lemons and the seeds shot out onto the floor, it reminded me of when I was sick and my sister was making tea for me. She was squeezing lemon juice into the cup and lemon juice squirted up into her eye. She was yelling and rubbing her eyes. It was so funny!

Nicole: Do you think that your connection helped you understand the book a little more?

Nicole reads aloud.

Tatiana: I guess. When you were reading, it didn't say that Julian thought his dad was funny, but I thought the story was funny because it was so funny when my sister got lemon juice in her eye.

Nicole: So your interpretation of the text is that the scene in Julian's kitchen was probably sort of funny with lemon seeds flying around? Great job, your connection gave you a deeper understanding of the text.

5. SEND STUDENTS TO PRACTICE

Nicole: In independent reading today, I want you to think about how you can connect what you read to your own experience. In reader's share, you'll share some of your connections with a partner. *(Students move off the rug and find places to read independently.)*

6. CONFER WITH INDIVIDUAL STUDENTS

Nicole checks her conference notes and sees that she has not yet conferred with Jessica this week.

Nicole:	Jessica, how is your reading going today?
Jessica:	It's okay.
Nicole:	Can you show me a place where you made a connection as you were reading?
Jessica:	I'm reading a book in the Magic Tree House series, *Dinosaurs Before Dawn*. It's a fantasy book and I can't really connect to it because I've never been in a tree house and I've never traveled through time.
Nicole:	No, I guess you haven't. It makes sense that you would find it difficult to make connections to a fantasy book because you haven't experienced anything like what you're reading about. But, I bet that there are some things in this book that are familiar. Does Jack or Annie remind you of anyone?
Jessica:	Well, I think I'm sort of like Jack. He loves to read and he carries a notebook in his backpack like I carry my writer's notebook.
Nicole:	So you can connect Jack's character to your own. Good readers relate to characters in books, not just settings or events. As you continue reading, see if Jack is like you in other ways.
Jessica:	Okay.

Nicole will check in with Jessica again tomorrow to see whether she is connecting to the book. As students begin to try out these strategies, it is important to give them frequent support and encouragement.

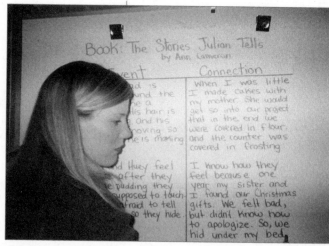

Stephanie models how to record connections.

FOLLOW-UP

Nicole will continue to read aloud, share connections, and encourage students to share their connections. After a few days, she will begin recording their connections on a large T-chart. (See sample left.) See page 47 for details.

Extend the Strategy
Making Connections to Other Texts

1. MAKE A CONNECTION

Nicole begins the lesson by reminding students of their work on making connections, so they understand that the lesson that follows is part of an ongoing study.

Nicole: For the past several days we've been talking about how good readers make connections between their lives and what they read to help their comprehension. Today we're going to add to the conversation. I want you to start thinking about connections between what you are reading now and what you've read in the past.

2. STATE THE PURPOSE OF THE STRATEGY

Nicole: I've noticed that a lot of you are reading books that you don't really connect to. Maybe the book takes place in a setting that is unfamiliar or has events that you've never heard of. Sometimes good readers connect what they are reading to other texts they've read in the past. Connecting to another text is another way to build understanding. Let's try it today.

3. MODEL THE STRATEGY

Nicole begins to read the third chapter of *The Stories Julian Tells*, entitled "Our Garden," in which Julian and his brother take a bath after working in their garden all day.

Nicole: As I was reading this part about Julian and Huey getting ready to take a bath, I remembered a conference I had with Laurie a few weeks ago.

Laurie: Are you talking about the *Mrs. Piggle-Wiggle* book I was reading because that's what I thought of, too!

Nicole: That's exactly what I was thinking. Tell the class about that story.

Laurie: In *Mrs. Piggle-Wiggle* there is this kid who refuses to take a bath. So Mrs. Piggle-Wiggle tells the kid's mom not to worry and to let him get all dirty. After a while he has a layer of dirt on him and his mom plants seeds in the dirt!

Purpose

To teach students to connect ideas between texts to enhance understanding

Materials and Preparation

Choose a read-aloud text and identify a part that is similar to another text the students know.

Nicole:	You connected *The Stories Julian Tells* to *Mrs. Piggle-Wiggle*. How do you think that helped you understand *The Stories Julian Tells*?
Laurie:	I don't know.
Nicole:	Which book had more description about what the kids looked like all caked in dirt?
Laurie:	*The Stories Julian Tells* didn't really describe the kids in much detail. *Mrs. Piggle-Wiggle* described a lot more about how that boy smelled and what he looked like.
Nicole:	Do you think that you have a better idea of what Julian and Huey looked like before their bath because you used some of the description from *Mrs. Piggle-Wiggle* to fill in?
Laurie:	I guess so.
Eryka:	I bet she did because I didn't even really pay attention to that part of the story. If I had read that book that Laurie read, I bet I would have thought more about that sentence.

4. Send Students to Practice

Nicole:	As you read today, think about other texts that you have read. But don't stop making personal connections. Just add another layer.

5. Confer With Individual Students

Nicole checks her conference notes and sees that she has not met with Dario this week. She also noticed that Dario has not been participating in class discussions of making connections; she wants to see how this strategy is working for him.

Nicole:	Hi Dario. How is your reading going today?
Dario:	Okay. I'm reading *The Meanest Thing to Say*. I've read a couple of these *Little Bill* books and I really like them.
Nicole:	That's great, Dario. I'm glad you've found a series that you enjoy. We've been talking about making connections for the past few days. How is that strategy going for you?
Dario:	In the beginning of the story, there's a new kid in class and it says that he starts making trouble on his first day. That reminded me of last year when we got a new boy in our class and he got in trouble on his first day! I couldn't believe it!

Nicole:	I'm glad you're making personal connections to this book. What about what we were talking about today, connecting what you are reading now to books you've read before?
Dario:	No, I didn't make any connections like that.
Nicole:	Well, let's read a bit together and talk about what's going on in your mind as you read.
Dario:	*(reads)* "This isn't how you play the game! You have to call me names. Call me stupid! Call me mean! I'm ugly!" Michael yelled.
	I laughed even harder. He was funny. "So?"
	Michael yelled even more.
Nicole:	I don't understand. Why is the character telling the story supposed to call Michael names? Why does the kid say 'so'?
Dario:	Little Bill asked his dad what he should do when Michael starts calling him names. His dad told him to say "So?" *(Dario flips back through pages.)* See, here's Little Bill's dad dancing around the kitchen talking about how he used to deal with bullies when he was in school. Hey! This reminds me of Julian's dad dancing around the kitchen when he was making the lemon pudding!
Nicole:	What did you just do, Dario?
Dario:	I connected this book to something else I've read!
Nicole:	Great job, Dario. Do you think you can continue to think about how this book is like other books you've read?
Dario:	Sure!

Nicole had to lead Dario to make this connection. She will continue to monitor his work to see whether he begins to make connections independently. She might use another book with a strong father figure in a guided reading group with Dario and others having a hard time with this strategy.

6. PAIR UP STUDENTS

Nicole asks each student to find a partner and to share the connections he or she made between two texts. She listens in to Shaun and Ozzie's conversation.

Shaun:	I was reading this book about coral reefs. It didn't remind me of anything I've read before, but it did remind me of a TV show I saw a while ago. They were talking about giant squid. They're huge and have really long arms.

Ozzie: Yeah! I saw something about how once a squid wrapped its arms around a submarine and crushed it!

Nicole: I'm sorry to interrupt. Shaun, how did the show you saw about giant squid help you to better understand the book about the coral reef?

Shaun: It just reminded me of it.

Nicole: It's really important that you remember to think about how the connection is helping your comprehension. Ozzie, were you able to make a connection to something else you've read?

Ozzie: I'm reading a book from the *Magic Tree House* series, so I connected this book to others in the series.

Nicole: Can you give me an example?

Ozzie: Well, in this book, *Night of the Ninjas*, an animal gets them out of trouble just like in *Dinosaurs Before Dark*.

Nicole: How do you think that helped your understanding?

Ozzie: When I read that the little mouse was squeaking, I knew that the mouse would help them because an animal always helps them get out of trouble.

Nicole: Great job, Ozzie. Shaun, does that make sense to you?

Shaun: Yeah, I'm thinking that this book on coral reefs is like a book I read about Australia a few weeks ago.

During the study of connections, it is imperative to remind students to think about how the connection improved their understanding. To keep track of this, Nicole asks her students to use a hopscotch chart, which is described on page 49.

MINI-LESSON Deepen the Strategy

Asking Questions Based on Connections

1. MAKE A CONNECTION

Nicole: We've been working on making connections. We know that good readers connect what they read to their own lives and they also connect what they read to other things they've read. Let's continue to learn about how good readers use connections to help them understand.

2. STATE THE PURPOSE OF THE STRATEGY

Nicole: As you read, do you ever wonder, "What's going to happen next?" or "Why did that happen?" Good readers ask lots of questions like that as they read. Today we're going to talk about using our connections to ask really good questions.

3. MODEL THE STRATEGY

Nicole reads aloud the final chapter of *The Stories Julian Tells*, "Gloria Who Might Be My Best Friend." At about the half-way point, Julian says to Gloria, "I wish you'd lived here a long time," to which Gloria replies, "I know the best way to make wishes."

Nicole: As I was reading this conversation between Julian and Gloria, I began to think about Andrew and Sharon in *Freckle Juice*. Remember how Sharon says that she knows how to make freckles? Well I'm going to use that connection to ask a question. "Will Gloria try to get Julian to pay for her wish recipe the way Sharon got Andrew to pay for his freckle recipe?" *(Writes the question on the dry-erase board.)* As I continue reading, I'm going to see if I can answer my question. *(Continues reading. In the story, Gloria does not try to trick Julian out of money. Instead they build and fly kites together.)*

Nicole: I think I found the answer to my question, and I came to understand the book even more. Gloria isn't like Sharon. She's kind. She genuinely wanted to help Julian make his wish come true. Julian and Gloria are really friends, not like Andrew and Sharon.

4. SEND STUDENTS TO PRACTICE

Nicole: During independent reading today, see if you can use the connections you make to ask questions about what will happen in the text. As you read on, try to answer your questions. After independent reading, we'll come together and talk about how it went.

5. CONFER WITH INDIVIDUAL STUDENTS

Nicole checks her conference notes and sees that she needs to have a conference with Eryka.

Nicole: Hi Eryka. How are you doing with your reading today?

Eryka:	Pretty good. I'm reading this book, *Balto and the Great Race*. I am making lots of connections to the *Time for Kids* article we read about the Ididerod race in Alaska.
Nicole:	Great job! You're using what you learned about sled dog racing in the *Time for Kids* article to help you understand *Balto*! Have you been able to ask any questions based on your connections like we talked about in read aloud today?
Eryka:	Not really.
Nicole:	Okay. Why don't you share a connection you've made and let's see if that connection leads you to a question.
Eryka:	*(Flips to page 29.)* Well, on this page it's talking about how it's really important that the driver of the sled take good care of the dogs' feet. I was thinking about how in the *Time for Kids* article, they talked about how some of the dogs push themselves so hard that they would die of exhaustion if their drivers didn't take care of them.
Nicole:	That's a great connection, Eryka. Think about that connection, what does it make you wonder about?
Eryka:	You mean about *Balto*?
Nicole:	Yes, or anything. Just think about that connection and tell me what's going on in your mind.
Eryka:	Well, the whole point of this book is that the dogs have to get to this town in Alaska really quickly to get medicine to some sick people. Maybe the sled driver won't rest the dogs well enough or take good enough care of their feet because they're in such a rush.
Nicole:	Do you have a question forming in your mind?
Eryka:	Sort of. I'm wondering if something bad will happen to the dogs because they're in such a rush.
Nicole:	Fantastic, Eryka! You used the connection you made to the *Time for Kids* article to ask if something bad will happen to the dogs. Can you write that question down and, as you read, try to find the answer?

6. SHARE AS A WHOLE GROUP

At the end of reading workshop, Nicole calls the class to the rug.

Nicole:	I asked you to try something really challenging today. I'd love to hear how that went.

Tatiana:	I didn't really think of any questions.
Dario:	Me either.
Nicole:	That's okay. As I said, this is hard work we're doing. Eryka had some success with this strategy today, Eryka will you share what we talked about today in our conference?
Eryka:	*(Shares the discussion she had with Nicole.)*
Nicole:	Thanks, Eryka. We'll continue to work on using connections to ask questions.

Although Nicole's students were unable to use this strategy independently, they made strides toward doing so. Nicole knows that she must continue to model and discuss this strategy. She might read another book in the Julian series, such as *More Stories Julian Tells*, to facilitate asking questions based on connections.

Assessment and Documentation

Talking about connections with the whole class, in small groups, and in conferences is important. We always ask, "How did your connection help you understand what you were reading?" By talking about connections this way, we get a sense of whether students are using them to make meaning from their reading. However, it's impossible to talk to every student every day. So we use assessment tools to capture students' reading experiences. Reviewing their responses to them allows us to determine whether students are progressing.

Connections T-Charts

Record Information as a Class: As we read *The Stories Julian Tells*, we share our own personal connections to the text, and encourage students to share their own. After a few days, we begin to record our connections on a T-chart as a class.

In the "Event in the Text" column, we write what happened that brought our connection to mind. In the "Connection" column, we write about the personal experience we had that connects to the event. This chart can be used for documenting both personal connections and connections to other texts.

Purpose

To have students record connections as they read independently

Materials and Preparation

Prepare a large T-chart on chart paper. Write "Event in the Text" at the top of the left-hand column and "Connection" at the top of the right-hand column. Photocopy enough blank T-charts for each student. (See Appendix 4.) Or students can make their own in their notebooks.

Naomi uses a pre-made T-chart to record the connections she makes during independent reading.

Name: Naomi	Date: 11\12

Connections T-Chart

Title: Nate The Great   Author: _____

Event in the Text	Connection
Nate Looks For a Picture For Annie. Annie aND Nate FiD Out that Annie's Brother PaiNTed The Picture.	I KNow How Annie FELt Because She Lost a Picture aND I Lost a Picture too. i have a Brother too aND MY Brother riteï MY Picture

Send Students to Practice: After a few days of recording connections on a class T-chart, we expect students to fill out individual T-charts based on their independent-reading books. (See sample above.)

Assess the Work: As we read over individual T-charts and conference with students about their connections, we keep these questions in mind:

- Can this student make personal connections to what she reads?
- Can this student describe the specific event that sparked the connection?
- Does the connection make sense?
- Can this student connect what she reads to other texts she has previously read?

Hopscotch Chart

"How Did Your Connections Help Your Comprehension?"

Purpose

To have students record how connections enhance their comprehension as they read independently

Record Information as a Class: Once students understand how to make connections, we want them to think about how their connections help them to understand what they read. We do this by recording on a hopscotch chart story events, our connections, and how our connections help us comprehend the text. We then invite students to share how their connections help them and add their responses to the chart.

Send Students to Practice: During readers respond, on blank hopscotch charts, students record events from and connections to their independent-reading books, and how those connections helped their comprehension.

Materials and Preparation

Prepare a large hopscotch chart on chart paper, labeled "How Did Your Connections Help Your Comprehension?" Photocopy enough blank hopscotch charts for each student. (See Appendix 5.) Or students can make their own in their notebooks.

Name: Stephanie and Class   Date: _____

How Did Your Connections Help Your Comprehension?

Title: The Stories Julian Tells   Author: Ann Cameron

Event	Connection
Julian has a new tooth growing in where his baby tooth still is.	Harry can connect with Julian because he has a new tooth coming in where his baby tooth still is.

How did this connection help your comprehension?
This connection helps Harry make a mind picture of Julian's tooth, and he can relate with Julian wanting to lose a baby tooth.

Event	Connection
Julian bites into an apple and says "ow!" He loses his tooth finally.	We can connect with Julian, because several of us have lost teeth by biting into food — especially apples!

How did this connection help your comprehension?
We understand how Julian feels. We also made a prediction that Julian would lose his tooth when the story said he was eating an apple.

Event	Connection
Julian is walking down his street feeling lonely when he sees a moving van and Gloria (a girl his age) outside of a house next door to his. The girl said hello and asked him to play.	Isaiah understands how Julian must feel because he recently moved and wondered if he'd make friends.

How did this connection help your comprehension?
Isaiah says that this connection is helping him understand the characters better. He is predicting they will become friends because Gloria said hello. Also, Julian won't be lonely anymore. He is making his prediction based on his own experience moving.

Stephanie and her class use this chart to determine how connections helped comprehension.

Assess the Work: As we read over individual hopscotch charts and conference with students about their connections, we keep these questions in mind:

- ◉ Can this student use connections to enhance her comprehension?

- ◉ Can this student explain how her connection helped her comprehension?

To have students ask and record questions based on connections, and read on for answers

Materials and Preparation

Prepare a large hopscotch chart on chart paper, labeled "Use Connections to Ask Good Questions". Photocopy enough blank hopscotch charts for each student. (See Appendix 6.) Or students can make their own in their notebooks.

Hopscotch Chart

"Use Connections to Ask Good Questions"

Record Information as a Class: Sophisticated readers use connections to ask good questions about the text. Then they read on for answers to their questions. So, as a class, during read aloud, we make connections, ask questions, and look for answers in the text. As we go, we write the information on the "Use Connections to Ask Good Questions" hopscotch chart.

Send Students to Practice:
During readers respond, students fill out their own photocopied charts based on their independent-reading books. They record connections, questions they raise, and answers they find in the text.

Assess the Work: As we read over individual hopscotch charts and conference with students about their connections, we keep these questions in mind:

⊚ Can this student ask questions based on connections?

⊚ Can this student find the answers to those questions?

Name: Class 5-0   Date: 10·18

Use Connections To Ask Good Questions

Title: *Class Share*   Author:

Connection	Question
While reading *The Fighting Ground*, Kosta made a connection to *My Brother Sam Is Dead*. In both books, a teenage boy wants to join the war but his brother doesn't want him to go.	Kosta wonders if Jonathan will steal his father's gun and run off to join the war the way Tim did in *My Brother Sam is Dead*.

Answers to the Question
(not yet answered)

Connection	Question
Morgan connected *My Brother Sam is Dead* to the *Journal of William Thomas Emerson*. In *The Journal...* Morgan learned that soldiers who deserted the army were killed.	Morgan wonders if that is how Tim will die, by deserting the army.

Answers to the Question
Tim is executed by the army but not for desertion. He is executed for stealing cattle even though he didn't actually steal the cattle.

Connection	Question

Answers to the Question

During a class share, Nicole's students explore questions that their connections raise.

Concluding Thoughts

Before we move on to another strategy, we make sure all students can make connections to what they read. We also make sure they can articulate how connections help them understand what they read. It might take more than one read aloud to get all students to this point. Once we move on, we can continue to support readers who struggle, in guided reading and reading conferences.

CHAPTER 5

Making Predictions

A

t an exciting part of a book or movie, we wonder, "What will happen next?" In our curriculum, we use that natural curiosity to help students understand what they read. We teach them to turn that simple question into a prediction.

To make a well-supported prediction, a student must use clues from the text and/or other texts to estimate what might happen. He must synthesize what is known about the text and infer what will happen based on what is known. In the process, he comes to understand the text more deeply as he pieces together that information.

Great Books
to Model
Predictions

Julie of the Wolves
by Jean Craighead
George (Harper & Row)

Hope's Crossing
by Joan Elizabeth
Goodman (Puffin
Books)

*Balto and the
Great Race*
by Elizabeth Cody
Kimmel (Random
House)

*The Magic Tree
House series*
by Mary Pope Osborne
(Random House)

OVERVIEW
of the Study

**We teach making well-supported predictions in
three phases, over four weeks. Specifically, we:**

- 🌀 introduce the strategy, teaching students to make predictions
  at various points in a text and then to note what actually
  happened.

- 🌀 extend the strategy, teaching students to use clues from the
  text to make predictions.

- 🌀 deepen the strategy, teaching students to keep their predictions in mind, recognize when they are no longer reasonable,
  and adjust them.

In this chapter, we include mini-lessons on each of these topics, as
well as tools for recording predictions that help assess students'
progress.

Choosing a Read-Aloud Text to Teach Making Predictions

To model making predictions, choose a text that you're confident will hold
students' attention, leave them wondering what will happen next, and make them
want to continue reading. Exciting adventures, fiction or nonfiction, work well
for us.

Tap into students' interests or curriculum topics that they seem to enjoy. For
example, while studying weather, we chose *The 21 Balloons* to capitalize on the
class' interest in hot-air balloons. During a study of the American Revolution,
fifth graders became fascinated by historical fiction about that time period. So, we
choose a well-written, exciting work of historical fiction.

For the following mini-lessons we use *Hope's Crossing*. In this book, Hope, the
daughter of a Continental captain from Connecticut, is kidnapped by British

soldiers and taken to Long Island. The story chronicles her journey back home, which involves a long stay in British-controlled New York City and a battle with smallpox.

Introduce the Strategy
Making Realistic Predictions

1. INTRODUCE THE LESSON

Nicole calls the class together.

Nicole: Does anyone know what the weather is supposed to be this weekend?

Morgan: I was watching the news with my dad last night and the weatherman said it was going to be nice.

Nicole: Good! I need to finish raking the leaves in my yard. Morgan, I'm glad you brought up the weatherman. What do we call what a weatherperson—or meteorologist—tells us about what the weather is going to be like?

Brendan: A guess?

Nicole: It's like a guess, but it's more than guess. Meteorologists take information from special instruments, and study maps and weather patterns, and then make a *prediction*. So a prediction is like a well-informed guess.

2. STATE THE PURPOSE OF THE STRATEGY

Nicole: Good readers make predictions just like meteorologists do. They think about everything that they know about the book and use that information to make realistic predictions. As I read this work of historical fiction, *Hope's Crossing*, we are going to work on making well-informed guesses, or predictions, about what we think will happen in the book.

Purpose

To show students how to make predictions while reading and to record what happens

Materials and Preparation

Pre-read your read-aloud choice. Prepare three predictions of what might happen in the story, only one of which should be reasonable. Also, prepare a T-chart on chart paper to record predictions during this and subsequent lessons. (See Appendix 7 for a sample T-chart.)

3. MODEL THE STRATEGY

Nicole: Before we begin, I'm going to make some predictions about what I think the book will be about. (*Displays the book's cover and reads aloud the description on the back.*) Based on the cover image, the description, and what I know about historical fiction, I came up with these three predictions.

Nicole writes her three predictions on the chart: I predict that *Hope's Crossing* will be about 1. Hope's father trying to rescue her. 2. Hope crossing Asia in a train. 3. the adventures Hope has after she's captured by the British.

4. PAIR UP STUDENTS

Nicole: Turn to the person next to you and talk about which predictions make sense. Which one shows that I used what I know about the book to make a realistic prediction? *(Listens in on Brendan and Kevin's conversation.)*

Brendan: The first prediction makes sense because the book could be about Hope's father trying to rescue her from the British. But the title is *Hope's Crossing*, so I wonder if the book will be more about Hope and not so much about her father.

Kevin: It might be, but remember *My Brother Sam Is Dead*? That wasn't really about Sam; it was about his brother, Tim. Maybe this will be more about Hope's father and not really about Hope.

Nicole: I like how you are using what you know about other works of historical fiction to decide which predictions are reasonable. *(Concludes that Kevin and Brendan understand realistic predictions, and moves on to Lauren and Allyson.)*

Lauren: I agree the last one makes the most sense. The second one doesn't make any sense at all!

Allyson: I know! After looking at the cover and reading the back of the book, what would make Ms. Outsen think that the book is going to be about traveling across Asia on a train?!

Nicole: Why doesn't that make sense, Allyson?

Allyson: The back of the book tells us that this is about a girl getting kidnapped during the American Revolution. It didn't say anything about Asia and they didn't even have trains then!

5. SHARE AS A WHOLE GROUP

Nicole: You all figured out that my second prediction doesn't make sense. There aren't any clues that this book has anything to do with Asia. I want to know what you think. You've heard the back-cover blurb, looked at the cover, and had time to discuss what the book might be about. Who can make a prediction about how this book might begin? After we make predictions, we'll read the first chapter and record how the book actually began.

Mackenzie: I think the book will start with Hope getting kidnapped.

Dylan: I think it will begin with the British soldiers planning to raid the town in Connecticut where Hope lives.

Nicole: Both of these predictions make sense. We know from the back of the book that Hope gets kidnapped and that the British raid a town in Connecticut. Now let's read the first chapter and see how the book really begins.

6. READ ALOUD

Nicole reads the first chapter of *Hope's Crossing*.

Nicole: What an exciting beginning! Now let's record what happened in the first chapter.

James: Mackenzie was right and Dylan was wrong!

Nicole: It's true that Mackenzie's prediction was correct. But being right is not really that important when you are making predictions. The most important thing is that your predictions be reasonable and that you can identify what really happened in the text. *(In subsequent mini-lessons, Nicole will chart students' predictions on a T-chart. [See sample right.])*

Nicole's model prediction and outcome chart.

7. SEND STUDENTS TO PRACTICE

Nicole: As you are reading today, try making realistic predictions. If you are reading a chapter book, you might want to do what we did today: Make a prediction before you begin a new chapter and then think about what happened after you've finished it. If you are reading a book that isn't broken into chapters, find a good place to pause and make a prediction. Don't forget to think about the outcome, too.

After students have practiced making realistic predictions for a few days, Nicole asks them to record their predictions and outcomes on photocopied T-charts. See page 61 for details.

MINI-LESSON

Extend the Strategy
Supporting Predictions

Purpose

To teach students to look for evidence in the text that supports their predictions

Materials and Preparation

Review your read-aloud choice. Display the T-chart used in earlier prediction lessons.

1. MAKE A CONNECTION

Nicole calls the class together.

Nicole: For the past few days we've been making realistic predictions during read aloud and independent reading. We've created this T-chart to help us keep track of our predictions.

2. STATE THE PURPOSE OF THE STRATEGY

Nicole: Today we are going to take predictions a step further. We are going to look for specific events that support our predictions, or back them up. As we make our predictions today, I will ask you to tell us *why* you think they're reasonable. You will use events from the book to support your opinions.

3. READ ALOUD AND MODEL THE STRATEGY

Nicole adds "with support" to the chart to remind students that they need to support predictions. She then reads a chapter in which Hope's kidnapper, Mr. Thomas, learns that his superiors are angry that he kidnapped a young girl. He and his wife discuss what to do with Hope.

Nicole: After reading this chapter, I predict that Hope is going to run away from the Thomas'. The book has given us a big clue that this might happen. Mrs. Thomas is planning on selling Hope to a trader. Hope vows that she will not be sold. She thinks to herself, "I wouldn't let them trade me like baggage. I'd run away in my shift if I had to." *(Adds her prediction with support to the chart.)*

4. SHARE AS A WHOLE GROUP

Nicole: I'd like to hear what you are thinking. Would anyone like to share a prediction and tell us what support the book gives you for it? Brendan?

Brendan: I predict that Mrs. Thomas is going to sell Hope into slavery.

Nicole: Why do you think that, Brendan?

Brendan: Well, Mrs. Thomas is the one that wants to get rid of Hope. She's the one that suggests to Mr. Thomas that they see that trader that won't ask any questions. Even though she expects Mr. Thomas to get rid of Hope, I don't think he will. I think Mrs. Thomas will be the one to do it.

Nicole: *(Adds Brendan's prediction with support to the chart.)* Great job, Brendan. You made a realistic prediction and have backed it up with events from the book. Does anyone else have a prediction?

Alex: I think that Mr. Thomas' mother, Mother Thomas, will die.

Nicole: Why do you think that?

Alex: She's old.

Nicole: Yes, but have there been any clues in the book that make us think that she's sick or going to die?

Alex: Not really. I just think she's going to die.

Nicole: Alex, I think you should continue to think about that prediction and if you find some specific events that support that idea, we'll put it up on the chart, okay?

5. SEND STUDENTS TO PRACTICE

Nicole: While you read today, think about any prediction that comes into your head. Think about the specific events that support that prediction.

6. CONFER WITH INDIVIDUAL STUDENTS

Nicole sits alongside Allyson, with whom she has not met this week.

Nicole: Hey Allyson, How's your reading going today? Are you making predictions?

Allyson: Yeah. I'm reading *Star Girl* by Jerry Spinelli. I predict that Star Girl and Leo, the narrator, are going to be friends, maybe boyfriend and girl-friend.

Nicole: Great job, Allyson. I'm wondering if you could support your prediction with specific examples from the book.

Allyson: (*Flips through the pages.*) I can't find the page right now, but I just get the feeling that Leo likes Star Girl.

Nicole: You are basing a prediction on a feeling you get from the book. That's great! What you need to work toward now is being able to find out what is giving you that feeling. Did Leo say something? Did he do something that showed you he was excited to be Star Girl's friend?

Allyson: Maybe I'll re-read a little and see if I can find out what gives me the idea that Leo likes Star Girl.

Nicole: That's a great plan, Allyson. You have a feeling about the book, which tells me you're understanding the book. But to *really* understand, you need to be able to support your hunches with specific details.

MINI-LESSON

Deepen the Strategy
Updating Predictions

1. MAKE A CONNECTION

Nicole calls the class together.

Nicole: As we've been reading *Hope's Crossing*, we've been talking about and recording predictions. We've also been recording outcomes, what really happened in the story, to determine if our predictions were correct.

Purpose

To help students keep their predictions in mind, recognize when they are no longer reasonable, and adjust them

Materials and Preparation

Review the class T-chart. Identify a prediction that is no longer valid and think of an alternate prediction. Keep the chart on display during the mini-lesson for student reference.

2. STATE THE PURPOSE OF THE STRATEGY

Nicole: Once we make a prediction about what might happen, it's easy to forget it. But today we're going to talk about the importance of reminding ourselves of our predictions and updating them when they are no longer reasonable. Readers keep their predictions in mind as they read because it helps them focus. They read on to see if what they think will happen does, or if the book will surprise them. Once a prediction is no longer reasonable, good readers adjust it to make it reasonable again.

3. MODEL THE STRATEGY

Nicole flips back though the class T-chart and reviews the predictions.

Nicole: As I look through, I realize that some of our early predictions might not be reasonable anymore. Take this one for example, "Mrs. Thomas will sell Hope to the slave trader." I'm not sure that prediction still makes sense since Hope and Mother Thomas have escaped from Mr. Thomas' house and are heading to New York. I think I have to update that prediction. I'm wondering about this character that Mother Thomas says will take them to New York City in his boat. He is a loyalist. He won't even put his boat in rebel waters. Maybe he'll find out that Hope is the daughter of a Patriot captain working for General Washington. Maybe he'll put her to work in his house. *(Records her updated prediction on the chart.)*

Nicole: Okay, let's keep reading. When we're done, we'll see if we need to update other predictions. *(Reads the next chapter of* Hope's Crossing.*)*

4. SHARE AS A WHOLE GROUP

Nicole: This story is exciting and full of surprises. Do we need to update other predictions since the story has gone in directions we didn't expect?

Brendan: Earlier in the book, I predicted that Mrs. Thomas would sell Hope into slavery. Now that Hope is in New York, I think I need to update that prediction.

Nicole: Okay, what do you think might happen now?

Brendan: They are looking for a way to get to Bedford. I think that they are going to be in New York for a long time.

Nicole: Why, Brendan?

Brendan: I was looking at Tabitha's prediction right in the beginning. She said that she thought the whole book would be about Hope trying to get home to her family like in *War Comes to Willie Freeman*. I'm beginning to think that she's absolutely right. So, if the whole book is going to be about Hope trying to get home, I think that she'll be in New York for a while trying to find a way to Bedford.

Nicole: Great prediction, Brendan, and great support! I really like how you are paying attention to your classmates' predictions.

5. SEND STUDENTS TO PRACTICE

Nicole: It's time for independent reading. Before you read today, look over the T-charts in your reading notebooks. As you read, keep your predictions in mind. And see if any of them need to be updated.

As with previous strategies, Nicole will ask students to begin recording their updated predictions after they have had experience thinking and talking about the strategy. See page 62 for details.

Assessment and Documentation

Throughout our study of predictions, we assess our students. We listen to what they share in whole-group discussions and conference with them regularly. Unfortunately, we cannot talk to each student every day. Therefore, we ask students to record their thinking as they make predictions, using a variety of tools.

T-Chart: Recording Predictions

*To record students'
predictions as they
read along with
supporting
evidence from
the text*

Name: Sergio .... Date: 6-18

Prediction T-Chart

Title: Super hoops trash talk   Author: Hank Herman

Prediction With Support	Outcome With Support
chapter #1 I think the chapter will be about that a teamate that won't **pass the** ball and he going to be a ball hog. so then the team won't be happy at the team. te because he is a ball hog.	**chapter #1** The outcome is that Jim was shouting at will because will was only stand ing and Jim was shouting out "pass or shoot" After will shot the ball. Will saw Nate with basket ball hoop→
chapter #2 I think this chapter will be about that Mr. Bowman will make the team practice alot until the game.	**chapter #2** The outcome is that the Banford Bulls figure out that Nate was going to Basket Ball camp. Jim had a idea of the Banford Bulls to coach themselves.

*Sergio recorded predictions and outcomes on sticky
notes and then transferred the notes to his chart.*

**Record
Information as a
Class:** After we spend
a few days talking about
the importance of making
realistic predictions and
supporting those predic-
tions with events from
the text, we begin to
chart our predictions and
the outcomes as a regular
part of our read aloud.

Materials and Preparation

*Make a large
T-chart on chart
paper. Write
"Prediction with
Support" at the top
of the left-hand
column and
"Outcome with
Support" at the top
of the right-hand
column. Photocopy
enough blank
T-charts for each
student. (See
Appendix 7.) Or
students can make
their own in their
notebooks.*

Send Students to Practice: Once students have had this whole-group
experience, we ask them to record predictions and outcomes during independent
reading, on photocopied T-charts, or in their notebooks. (See sample above.)

Assess the Work: As we review students' predictions and outcomes, and
conference with students, we keep these questions in mind:

- ◎ Can this student make realistic predictions?
- ◎ Can this student support predictions with events or clues from the book?
- ◎ Can this student recognize and describe the outcomes of their predictions?

T-Chart: Updating Predictions

Purpose

To reflect on early predictions and adjust them if necessary

Materials and Preparation

You'll need the filled-out T-chart from the activity above, with an added column, entitled "Updated Predictions." Prepare paper strips for students to add the same column to their individual charts. Photocopy Prediction/Outcome/Updated Prediction charts for students use. (See Appendix 8.)

Record Information as a Class: After reading several chapters of a book, we go back and re-read early predictions. Some of these predictions are no longer reasonable. They need to be updated. We add a third column to our

Name: Taylor   Date: 11/13

Update Predictions

Title: Torn Thread   Author: Anne Isaacs

Prediction	Outcome	Updated Prediction
I predict Rachel will get very sick because lately Rachel has been coughing, having fevers and not being able to breath.	Rachel got the nettles but it wasn't because of the symptoms she had. At night and throughout the day it is hard for her to breath	I predict Rachel will continue to have lung problems because she is constantly coughing and wheezing.

Taylor updates his predictions about Torn Thread.

chart and record our updated predictions. We then invite students to share their updated predictions during read aloud.

Send Students to Practice: After students have had lots of experience practicing this as a group, we ask them to review their own predictions from their independent-reading books, and update them as necessary. We distribute paper strips that students tape onto their Prediction/Outcome charts. (See sample above.)

As they make new predictions, they use a three-column Prediction/ Outcome/Updated Prediction chart, which provides a convenient way for students to record, review, and update their predictions from their independent-reading books.

Assess the Work: As we review students' predictions and outcomes and conference with students, we keep these questions in mind:

◎ Can this student recognize a prediction that is no longer reasonable?

◎ Can this student update a prediction to make it reasonable?

Time Line of Predictions

Purpose

To assess students' comprehension of the whole book

Materials and Preparation

Make a model time line of predictions, based on the read-aloud book. Students will need large sheets of construction paper, lined paper, and their completed Prediction/Outcome/Updated Prediction charts.

Create a Model Time Line: It's important to assess students' comprehension of the overall text. Traditionally, we do so by assigning book reports. Making a time line of predictions is a great alternative because it asks students to review all the good thinking and predicting they did as they read, and allows them to represent their reading.

To create the model time line, we review the class T-chart and find several predictions and outcomes that exemplify good use of the strategy. We rewrite the predictions and outcomes in full sentences, using lots of detail. Then we put the information in chronological order to capture the progression of the book. (See photo below.) We share the model with the whole class, explaining how we created it and how it represents all the good thinking we've put into the book.

Send Students to Create Their Own Time Lines: As students finish their independent-reading books, we invite them to celebrate their accomplishment by creating a prediction time line of their own, during reader respond time. We leave the model on display, as a reference.

Assess the Work: As you review students' time lines, keep this question in mind: Did this student include complete and well-supported predictions with outcomes?

Concluding Thoughts

We teach children how to make realistic predictions, support those predictions, review them, and change them if necessary. Our goal is to get students to think more deeply about a text by articulating how clues lead them to predictions. Once most of them are able to do so, we introduce a new study.

Nicole made this model Map of Predictions based on MY BROTHER SAM IS DEAD by James and Christopher Collier. It shows destinations of characters, which is one way of compiling important predictions across an entire book.

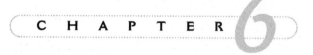
Getting to Know Characters

When we understand a character in a book, we see the story through that character's eyes and essentially step into his or her shoes. We can predict how the character will act in certain situations and connect deeply when changes happen to him or her. Our comprehension of the text becomes stronger as a result.

We show students how to use what they know about a character to strengthen their comprehension. When we teach students that a character's actions can be used as clues to understand his or her traits, and that traits can change and can give insight into what a character will do next, students become more strategic readers.

OVERVIEW
of the Study

We teach getting to know characters in three phases, over four weeks. We model each phase in mini-lessons and give support and feedback to students as they attempt the strategy independently. Specifically, we:

- ◎ introduce the strategy, teaching students to pay attention to a character's actions as a way to understand him or her.

- ◎ extend the strategy, teaching students how to make generalizations about a character's personality, based on his or her actions.

- ◎ deepen the strategy, teaching students how a character's traits give insight into what that character will do next.

When students see a character as an essential part of the story, as a tool to understand what they are reading, their level of comprehension deepens.

Choosing a Read-Aloud Text to Teach Getting to Know Characters

Before we begin the study, we choose a read-aloud text. We look for books that:

- ◎ have a relatively simple story line.

- ◎ are predictable, perhaps a title in a familiar series.

- ◎ show evidence of character development.

- ◎ interest students.

Day of the Dragon King by Mary Pope Osborne, which is part of her Magic Tree House series, is wonderful for teaching character. In it, Jack and Annie travel back to ancient China to save a legend, which is threatened by the Dragon King who

Great Books to Model Getting to Know Characters

Amber Brown series
by Paula Danziger
(Putnam)

26 Fairmont Avenue series
by Tomie DePaola
(Putnam)

Monkey Island
by Paula Fox (Orchard Press)

Cobble Street Cousins series
by Cynthia Rylant
(Aladdin)

has ordered the burning of all books—including the one containing the legend. While on their adventure, Jack and Annie approach their adventures in consistent ways, making it easy to pinpoint their character traits. Also, since the book is part of a series and contains a predictable story line, it is a good choice.

Introduce the Strategy
Keeping Track of a Character's Actions

1. INTRODUCE THE LESSON

Stephanie calls the whole class together.

Stephanie: Lately, I have been thinking about how nice it is to have friends that you know so well, you know what they will say or how they will act. Ms. Outsen and I are friends like that. I know that she loves to cook. I know her favorite books. I know what things will make her sad or happy. And, at times, I can predict what she will do before she does it. Do you have friends like that?

(Several students nod.)

Stephanie: When I read a book, I often form a connection with the characters. Usually, I can predict what they will do next, or I feel sad if something bad happens to them. Do you remember when I read *A Taste of Blueberries* and I cried at the end?

(Several students nod.)

Stephanie: That is a perfect example. I'd say I get to know characters like close friends.

2. STATE THE PURPOSE OF THE STRATEGY

Stephanie: Knowing characters like good friends is something good readers do. To get to know a character that well, you need to observe and note his or her actions. Today, we are going to read *Day of the Dragon King* by Mary Pope Osborne. While reading, we are going to keep track of the things that Jack and Annie do, their actions. After reading, we are going to note the things that each character does to see if it helps us understand him or her better.

Purpose

To introduce note taking as a way to understand a character better

Materials and Preparation

Pre-read your read-aloud choice. Make note of a character's actions that will help students understand him or her better. Have chart paper available to record the character's traits on a web.

3. MODEL THE STRATEGY

Stephanie reads the first chapter of *Day of the Dragon King*. After reading, she pauses and discusses briefly what the chapter was about.

Stephanie: Now that we have discussed what the chapter is about, let's think about Jack and Annie's actions. What things did these characters do that help us understand them better? *(Gives students some think time. Nobody answers.)*

Stephanie: I noticed at the beginning that Jack kept worrying about their trip before they had even left. For instance, in this part here. *(Refers back to a passage.)* Jack's mom tells them to have fun in China, and Jack thinks to himself, "fun?" Then he tells Annie that their adventures are always very scary. I think that this part is important because it helps us understand how Jack feels about the trip. I am going to add this to our web of the things Jack does that help us understand him better. *(Adds the detail to Jack's web.)*

Sergio: Oh, but Annie did not act scared. She was talking all the way to the tree house. She asked Jack what the weather was like in China.

Katrina: Then she said that she couldn't wait to meet the animals or people who would help them on their adventure.

Stephanie: True. Annie did say those things. Let's add that information to our web of Annie. *(Adds the detail to Annie's web.)*

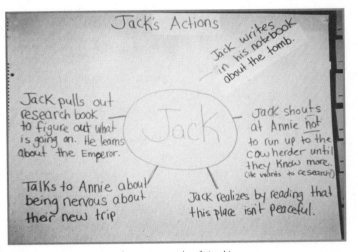
Stephanie creates a character web of Jack's actions.

Felicia: One thing that Jack did was carry the China research book. He always carries the books.

Anthony: Jack is pretty much scared. But he is the one who pointed at the book and said to go there.

Stephanie: Good point, Anthony. At the end of the chapter, Jack is acting in a different way than he did at the beginning of the chapter. We will have to watch and see if this is something he always does. *(Adds the students' details to the webs.)* These are all good examples of the things that these characters did. As we continue to read this book, we will keep track of the things Jack and Annie do and see if it helps us understand them better.

4. SEND STUDENTS TO PRACTICE

Stephanie: Today, as you read independently, pay attention to the characters' actions. Remember that observing the things your characters do, their actions, will help you get to know them like good friends. I will check in to see how it is going.

5. CONFER WITH INDIVIDUAL STUDENTS

Stephanie sits down next to Felicia, who is a strong reader but often gravitates towards making only personal connections with texts. Stephanie wants to check in with her to see whether she is keeping track of her characters' actions.

Stephanie: Felicia, what are you reading today?

Felicia: I am reading *B-E-S-T Friends*, a New Kids at Polk Street School book. I just finished Chapter 2.

Stephanie: Have you read any of the other New Kids books?

Felicia: No, this is my first one. I like it.

Stephanie: Are you getting to know a character well?

Felicia: Yeah, Stacy. I think she seems nice. She is like me.

Stephanie: Are there certain actions Stacy is doing that make you think that?

Felicia: Stacy is always singing to herself. She spins her plate at dinner and then eats the food that stops in front of her. I'd love to do that. My mom would hate it, though. Stacy's mom doesn't like it. She also has an older sister who picks on her just like me. She doesn't get too mad, either.

Stephanie: *(Notes that Felicia is using her personal connection to form her opinion of Stacy rather than the evidence in the text.)* Seems as if you are really connecting with this text, and keeping track of what you are learning about Stacy. But I have a question. Does the fact she spins her plate or that she has an older sister like you make you think that she is nice?

Felicia: No, I guess not. We're just a lot alike, so maybe she is nice, too.

Stephanie: Sometimes when we read, we realize that we have similarities to characters. You and Stacy both like spinning plates and have older sisters. It is easy to confuse our similarities with what the character does. Spinning her plate and not liking the way her sister treats her doesn't tell us that Stacy is nice. They might show that she is playful and sensitive, but we need to read more to be sure of that. Keep paying attention to the things Stacy does. *(Plans to support Felicia in guided reading by helping her keep track of a character's actions.)*

6. SHARE AS A WHOLE GROUP

Stephanie: Today, when I was conferencing, I noticed that some of you tried observing the characters in your books and noting the things they did. Let's share some of the things you noticed.

Andy: I am reading a Cam Jansen book, *The Mystery of the Babe Ruth Baseball*. In these books, Cam always goes "click." Today she saw a boy in a green jacket touching the baseball and she went "click." Later the ball was gone. I think Cam knows the boy took the ball and that is why she remembers it. I like how she always goes "click" to help her solve the case.

Felicia: I read *B-E-S-T Friends*. Stacy has to be the new girl's partner and she is not so happy about it. She was supposed to be Jiwon's partner. The new girl, Annie, is messy, whistles from her teeth, and won't listen to Stacy when she tries to show her what they do in class. It makes Stacy mad.

Stephanie: How do you know she is not happy about being the new girl's partner?

Felicia: Because she keeps talking to herself about the new girl. At the end she says that Annie is a pest.

Stephanie: You have all really paid close attention to the things that characters in your books do. It sounds as if you are all getting to know them like close friends. *(Notes that Felicia took her advice and found evidence to support the character's actions, but will still support her in guided reading and follow-up conferences.)*

MINI-LESSON

Extend the Strategy

Defining Characters' Traits Based on Actions

1. MAKE A CONNECTION

Stephanie calls the class together.

Stephanie: Over the past few days, we have been keeping track of Jack and Annie's actions. This information has helped us understand the types

Purpose

To teach students how to make generalizations about a character's personality

Materials and Preparation

Pre-read the chapter from your read-aloud choice. Make notes of a character's actions that translate into clear examples of his or her traits. Display the webs you have been creating as a class.

69

of things they do. Do you feel you are getting to know them by observing them?

Anthony: I do. I really like Jack because he carries a notebook around and loves to write in it. He writes what he researches. I do that too.

Winnie: I think Annie is fun.

Stephanie: What do you mean by fun?

Winnie: Well, she is always happy. She is not scared. She likes their adventures.

2. STATE THE PURPOSE OF THE STRATEGY

Stephanie: You are getting to know Jack and Annie really well. You are naming their traits. Traits are generalizations based on a consistent behavior or action. For instance, if you knew someone who could never remember where they put their keys, constantly left their homework at home, or always arrived late, you would probably say that person's character trait is "forgetful."

Felicia: Oh, I get it. My cousin always tells good jokes, and makes me laugh even when I am sad. So my cousin is funny.

Stephanie: Right. Today, as I read Chapter 4 to you, take note of Jack and Annie's actions. Then we are going to look at our webs and see if we can find some consistent actions that help us define Jack and Annie's traits. *(Reads Chapter 4.)*

3. MODEL THE STRATEGY

Stephanie: Now that we have read four chapters, we have a good amount of information to help us begin looking for traits. One thing that I noticed is that Jack is nervous a lot. For example, he was nervous in Chapter 1, when they were just talking about going to China. He walked slowly to the silk weaver, while Annie ran. And, at the beginning of this chapter, his heart is pounding out of control as they hide in the cart. I'd have to say that these examples prove that one of Jack's traits is nervousness. *(Writes "Nervous" on Jack's web and puts a box around it. She then connects the word to the actions that prove her point.)* When naming a trait, it is important to use the actions as evidence. Now, let's look at Annie's web. *(Flips through the book.)* I am noticing that in this part, Annie runs up to the silk weaver and smiles. Here, she waves at the cow herder and smiles. Here, she tells Jack how excited she is to be in China. I would say that a trait that defines Annie is happiness. *(Adds "Happy" to Annie's web.)*

4. Pair Up Students

Stephanie: Now, I'd like you to pair up and continue naming Jack and Annie's traits. Turn and talk to your partner about what traits you think define Jack and Annie. Remember to be able to prove your thoughts with actions as your evidence. We will share in a couple of minutes. *(Walks around the room, listens in to the discussions, and notes how students are doing.)*

5. Share as a Whole Group

Stephanie: Now, I'd like a few partners to share the traits they think define Jack or Annie and why.

Katrina: Well, Jack loves to research books. He always looks for the answers to his questions in a book. Like, when they first arrived and he tried to figure out what he was seeing.

Stephanie: How could we name that action as a trait?

Katrina: Either that he's smart or that he is a researcher.

Sergio: Annie is smart, too. She just does it differently. She learns because she is curious about the world and people around her. She ran right up to the silk weaver. She talks to the cow herder and the scholar.

Stephanie: What do you think those actions tell us about Annie? Can we turn that information into a trait?

Sergio: Yeah, I'd say it means she is curious. It could also mean she is friendly.

Stephanie: Those are both great traits. You can name any trait what you want, as long as there is evidence.

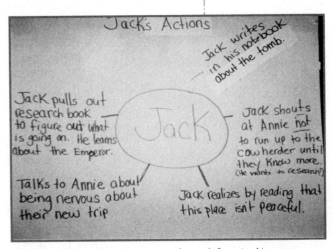

Stephanie uses the character web to define Jack's traits.

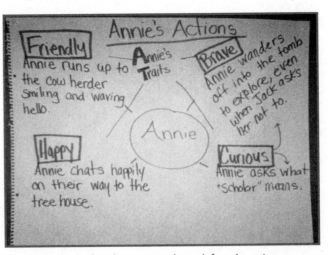

Stephanie uses the character web to define Annie's traits.

71

Andy: They are both kind because they help Morgan and people they meet on their adventures.

Stephanie continues to chart the students' examples and reasons for them. After students have recorded character traits in a whole group for a few days, she asks them to try it in their independent-reading books. See page 75 for details.

6. SEND STUDENTS TO PRACTICE

Stephanie: Today, as you read independently, pay attention to the characters' actions. Try to push yourself to look deeper at their actions and see if you can begin to define your characters' traits by using their actions as evidence. I will check in with you to see how it is going.

MINI-LESSON

Deepen the Strategy
Using Character Traits to Make Predictions

Purpose

To teach students that a character's traits give us insight into what the character will do next

Materials and Preparation

Pre-read later chapters in your read-aloud choice. Flag good points to stop and make predictions about what the character will do next.

1. MAKE A CONNECTION

Stephanie calls the class together.

Stephanie: We have been working hard on understanding Jack and Annie. By noting their actions and defining their traits, I feel I am getting to know them like good friends. I want to keep reading to figure out what they will do next. When we left off yesterday, Jack and Annie found themselves in a room filled with soldiers. After we stopped reading, I kept thinking about what they will do to get themselves out of this predicament.

(Several students nod.)

2. STATE THE PURPOSE OF THE STRATEGY

Stephanie: By thinking about what Jack and Annie will do next, I am doing what good readers do: predicting. Good readers use what they know about a character to help them make predictions. Today, I would like us to use what we know about Jack and Annie's traits to help us make predictions about what we think the characters will do next. When I read

Chapter 8, I will stop every so often and make a prediction. Then you will talk with partners and make your own predictions.

3. MODEL THE STRATEGY

Stephanie: The title of this chapter is "The Tomb." Well, we now know that they are located in a tomb. Based on the fact that we decided that Annie is positive, trusts people, and enjoys adventure, I don't think she will be too scared. Being nervous is a character trait we noted about Jack. I think that he is going to be scared. Let's read and find out. *(Reads the chapter's first two pages. Annie reveals herself to the soldiers while Jack holds his breath. Annie pulls a soldier's nose and points out to Jack that they are fake. She thinks this is exciting, like a museum. Jack thinks it is spooky.)* I'm glad that we noticed those traits about Jack and Annie because it did help us understand. Jack is scared and Annie is excited! Now, what do you think Jack or Annie will do next and why?

Winnie: Jack is definitely going to look up where they are in the research book that Morgan gave them about China. He always does that.

Sergio: Annie will be more curious about the statues and investigate. Remember how she ran straight up to the cow herder and the silk weaver?

Stephanie: Good predictions for what we think the characters will do next. Let's read and find out. *(Reads the next two pages. Jack reads his research book and learns that they are in the Dragon King's tomb, for which the king had 7,000 life-size soldier statues made from clay. Annie wanders off into the statues. She calls to Jack to look closely at the faces because they are all different.)* Great predictions. Jack did research and Annie did explore. He is a researcher and she is curious. What do you think will happen next?

Anthony: Jack will write about what he is learning. He always does that when he is excited.

4. PAIR UP STUDENTS

Stephanie: *(Reads the next page. Jack pulls out his notebook and writes about the statues. Then Annie points out to Jack that they are lost and don't know how to get out of the tomb.)* Now, pair up and talk with your partner about what will happen next. What will Annie and Jack do to get out of the maze of statues? Make sure you tell what trait or past action is helping you make your prediction. *(Walks around the room, listens in on discussions, and notes how the students are applying the strategy.)*

5. CONFER WITH PARTNERS

Stephanie sits down next to Lindsay and Eric. Both students were quiet during her lesson, and she wants to make sure they understand.

Lindsay: I bet Jack will get really scared again. Annie won't be scared.

Stephanie: That is a good prediction, but why do you think that Jack will get scared again and Annie won't?

Lindsay: I am not so sure. I just think that.

Stephanie: Is being scared a trait of Jack's? Bravery, a trait of Annie's?

Lindsay: Yes.

Stephanie: Can you think of something specific Jack would do because he gets scared, or Annie would do because she is not?

Lindsay: *(Shakes her head.)*

Eric: Well, we learned at the beginning of the book that animals or things usually save them. Annie always says that. She'll save them somehow. Something has to save them! Jack will probably not go any further, and Annie will search out something to help them get back to the tree house.

Stephanie: Good use of past actions, Eric. What helped you remember the detail?

Eric: I reread the action chart, and that helped me a lot.

Stephanie: Thanks for sharing that strategy with Lindsay and me. *(Gathers the class together, and they read the last remaining pages.)*

6. SEND STUDENTS TO PRACTICE

Stephanie: Today, as you read independently, try to make predictions. Remember to use the traits that you know about your character to help. Some students use a character's past actions to help them think ahead. That is a good strategy, too. I will check in with you to see how it is going. After independent reading we will have a share about how this strategy is helping you.

After students have made predictions based on traits as a whole group for a few days, Stephanie asks them to role-play their predictions. See page 76 for details.

Assessment and Documentation

Modeling how to get to know characters, and allowing students to practice on their own, are important. Over time, students begin to think like characters, understand their traits, predict their actions, and articulate how and why characters change.

It's also important to give students opportunities to respond to the strategy, to demonstrate and deepen their understanding of it. Along with conference notes, their responses, both oral and written, provide excellent records of students' progress. Here are some of the ways our students responded to getting to know a character.

Character Webs

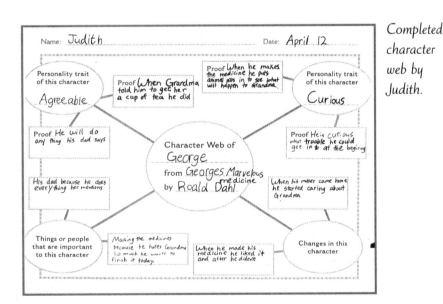

Completed character web by Judith.

Purpose

To explore the connection between a character's actions and his or her traits

Materials and Preparation

Prepare blank webs. For younger children, photocopy and distribute the web template. (See Appendix 9.) Older children can use the same template or make their own in notebooks.

Record Information as a Class: During read aloud, we keep track of the characters using a web on a class chart. We write in the character's traits as well as his or her actions that led us to assign those traits.

Send Students to Practice: After a few days of group work, students practice on their own. On a photocopied web template or in their notebooks, they record important actions of a character from their independent-reading books. From there, they use those actions to determine the character's traits.

75

Assess the Work: While conferring with a student about his or her response, keep the following questions in mind to help you assess understanding:

◎ Can this student keep track of a character's actions?

◎ Can this student determine traits based on those actions?

Role Play

Purpose

To help students think like their character by using what they know about him or her to act out a scene that has happened or may happen

Materials and Preparation

Make a transparency of a passage from your read-aloud book.

Model the Activity: Role-playing is a wonderful way for students to get to know a character and use that knowledge to make predictions. So, to prepare for role playing, be sure to choose a part of your read-aloud book that contains dialogue and a predictable situation.

First, we read aloud a page from the book and ask students to predict what the characters will do and why. Then we ask what the characters might say in the next scene. Students usually come up with a variety of ideas. We act out what might happen next, based on those ideas, possibly inviting a child to role-play with us. Then we read on to confirm our prediction.

Pair Up Students: The next time we do this activity, we might show the beginning of a scene on the overhead, ask students to read it, and have them role-play their predictions in pairs. We ask a few partners to share with the group and assess how it is helping them understand the strategy. Once a few partners have role-played, we read on as a class to see what actually happens.

Send Students to Practice: After a few days of role-playing during read aloud, we expect students to try it during independent reading. Students work in partners, reading parts of their books that contain important actions of a character and then acting out what they feel will happen next.

Assess the Work: When conferring with students about their role-playing, keep the following questions in mind:

◎ Is this student aware of the character's traits?

◎ Can this student make predictions based on the character's traits?

Letters to Characters

Model the Activity: Another way to capture what students have learned about a character over the course of a book is to have them write letters to characters. These letters provide evidence of the extent to which students understood the character and, therefore, make excellent assessment tools.

We model this activity on chart paper after we finish a read-aloud book. We discuss with students that a letter should include details from the book that show that we understand the character, that support our opinions, or that bring forth questions.

Send Students to Practice: After a few days of modeling, we expect students to write letters to a character from their independent-reading books. (We may give them a chance to write letters to a character from the read-aloud book beforehand, depending on their needs.) We remind them to include details from the book that show that they understand the character, support their opinions, and raise ask questions that relate to the character. (See sample below.)

Assess the Work: When conferring with a student about his or her letter, keep the following questions in mind:

- ◎ Can this student define the character's traits?

- ◎ Does this student understand the character?

- ◎ Can this student provide evidence from the book that helps him or her form opinions and ask questions?

Closing Thoughts

Studying a character is a wonderful way to deepen comprehension of and extend interactions with a book. If our students had needed more models, we might have chosen a book with a more complex story line and character, such as *Sable* by Karen Hesse. We would also support them by addressing characters in guided reading, shared reading, and other components of our program.

Purpose

To have students express their thoughts, opinions, and questions about a character by putting them in writing

Materials and Preparation

Have chart paper and markers to model the activity.

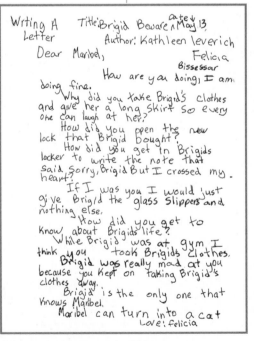

Letter to a character by Felicia.

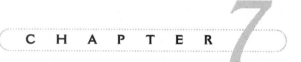
Creating Mind Pictures

When good readers read, they envision the text in their minds. This strategy has many names. In *Mosaic of Thought* (Heinemann), Ellin Keene and Susan Zimmerman refer to it as "using sensory images." In *Strategies That Work* (Stenhouse), Stephanie Harvey and Anne Goudvis refer to it as "visualization." We call it "making mind pictures." When readers pay attention to elements such as setting, character, mood, and details, the text almost comes alive. They can "see" the author's message. Mind pictures provide them with a full, vivid image of the text.

Although many students subconsciously make mind pictures as they read, they might not know that pictures can help their comprehension. We need to teach them to pay attention to those pictures. They need to be taught to use details to visualize a more complete image of the text. They need to be taught to stop when they are unable to visualize. If we do this, students are more likely to understand the meaning of what they read.

OVERVIEW
of the Study

We teach this strategy in three phases, which gradually lead children to make mind pictures independently. Specifically, we:

- introduce the strategy, teaching students to pay attention to the images that come into their minds as they read.

- extend the strategy, teaching students to locate details that confirm their understanding of the text.

- deepen the strategy, teaching students to synthesize many mind pictures into a composite picture to arrive at the central meaning of the text.

By teaching making mind pictures along this continuum, at a pace students can handle, we break a complex and often subconscious process into manageable steps. In this chapter, we provide mini-lessons on those topics, as well as ideas for helping students apply them when they read independently.

Great Books to Model Getting Mind Pictures

Half Moon Inn
by Paul Fleishman
(HarperCollins)

Shark Lady: The Adventures of Eugenie Clark
by Ann McGovern
(Four Winds Press)

The Blue Hill Meadows
by Cynthia Rylant
(Scholastic)

Choosing a Read-Aloud Text to Teach Creating Mind Pictures

Before we begin the study, we find a read-aloud text that lends itself to making mind pictures. We look for books that contain vivid details and concrete descriptions. We avoid books with lots of metaphors or other kinds of figurative language, which might make visualizing difficult. *The Chalk Box Kid* by Clyde

Bulla is an excellent text to introduce, extend, and deepen the strategy. In this story, nine-year-old Gregory moves to a new neighborhood. To ease his loneliness, he begins to draw a mural of a garden on the walls of a burned-out building behind his house. One day in school, he tells his classmates about his "garden" but fails to mention it is drawn in chalk. When his classmates follow him home, they call him a liar. But his teacher, parents, and special classmate, Ivy, begin to see Gregory in a new way when they see what he's created.

Introduce the Strategy
Finding Mind Pictures

Purpose

To make students cognizant of mind pictures during read aloud

Materials and Preparation

Pre-read your read-aloud choice. Identify a scene in the first chapter that paints a vivid mental picture for you.

1. INTRODUCE THE LESSON

Stephanie sits in front of her class, poised to read aloud *The Chalk Box Kid* by Clyde Bulla. Before she begins, she explains the strategy.

Stephanie: How many of you read or heard the story *James and the Giant Peach* before you saw the movie?

(Several students raise their hands.)

Stephanie: Okay. Was anyone disappointed when they saw the movie? Did the characters look right to you or had you imagined them differently?

Ozzie: I read that book with my mom. I had imagined the characters to look a certain way and dress a certain way. The old aunts especially. Then I saw the movie and they didn't look anything like how I imagined them.

Stephanie: So, Ozzie, you had made your own "movie" in your head as you heard the story, and the movie in the theater didn't match up?

Ozzie: Yeah.

Stephanie listens as many other students share stories of movies or TV shows in which characters or settings were depicted in ways they hadn't expected.

2. STATE THE PURPOSE OF THE STRATEGY

Stephanie: As you all read and heard those stories, you did something that good readers do all the time: visualize. Good readers make pictures in their minds as they read. When readers make mind pictures, they understand the text more deeply because they can see it. They are a part of it.

Eryka: I know what you mean. I'm reading *Junie B. Jones Has a Monster Under Her Bed* and I can picture her so clearly in my head. It's like she's real!

Stephanie: Exactly, Eryka. When characters and stories come alive in your imagination, you understand them better than when you can't really picture them. As I read our new read aloud, *The Chalk Box Kid* by Clyde Bulla, we're going to work on paying attention to our mind pictures so that the story can come alive. I'm going to share my images with you and you'll share them with me and with each other.

3. MODEL THE STRATEGY

Stephanie reads the first chapter of *The Chalk Box Kid* without stopping. When she finishes, she closes her eyes and describes the scene.

Stephanie: I can see Gregory's room, every inch. His family just moved into the house, so there isn't anything on the walls. There is only a bed in the corner. The bed has only one pillow, and no headboard or comforter. There is a window across from the bed, looking out on the street. There aren't any curtains yet. In the corners, I can see dust balls because this room hasn't been swept for a long time. The walls seem gray to me. Maybe they're just dirty or maybe there just isn't much light in the room and it's nighttime. Gregory is sitting on his bed looking around. He's smiling. *(She stops, opens her eyes, and looks at the class.)*

4. SHARE AS A WHOLE GROUP

Stephanie: Let's share the images some of you got in your heads as I read. I'll give you a few seconds to remember the images and then we'll hear from three people.

Xiao saw Greg sitting alone in his room looking out the window at the dark street. Belinda saw a mattress on the floor because she doesn't think the family has gotten a bed for Gregory yet. Eryka saw a scene identical to Stephanie's, which is a warning sign. Stephanie will conference with Eryka during independent reading to see if she can make mind pictures on her own.

5. SEND STUDENTS TO PRACTICE

Stephanie: As you read independently today, pay attention to the pictures you have in your mind. Let them become clear. During reader's share, we'll talk about some of those pictures. *(Students disperse around the classroom for independent reading.)*

6. CONFER WITH INDIVIDUAL STUDENTS

Stephanie sits down next to Eryka.

Stephanie: Eryka, you shared two really interesting things during read aloud today. First, you described your experience reading a Junie B. Jones book. I thought to myself, "Wow, Eryka makes great mind pictures!" Then you shared your mind picture from *The Chalk Box Kid*'s first chapter, and it sounded a lot like mine. So I thought I'd come check in with you. Can you tell me more about what making mind pictures is like for you as a reader?

Eryka: It's so weird. When I'm reading to myself, I really see what's going on in the book. Like I told the class, I can see the character of Junie B. Jones. But, when you were reading to us, I couldn't really do that. I didn't really get a picture in my mind until you described your picture and then I could see it.

Stephanie:: Eryka, it sounds to me like you make mind pictures well when you read independently, but have a harder time when you are listening. Will you share that experience in reader's share today? I bet other readers in the class had a similar experience. Maybe we can have a guided-reading group to work on that. I'm going to make a note here next to your name.

Eryka watches as Stephanie writes, "Visualizes well while reading independently, harder when listening to read aloud." After a few days of creating and talking about mind pictures as a whole group, Stephanie asks students to sketch their mind picture while reading independently. See page 88 for details.

See page 88 for details.

MINI-LESSON
Extend the Strategy
Pinpointing the Language That Creates Mind Pictures

1. MAKE A CONNECTION

Stephanie calls the class together.

Stephanie: We know that good readers get images in their minds as they read, and that these images can help them see the scenes. We have learned that making mind pictures can help us understand better what we are reading. Still, I am curious about what an author does that helps a reader make a mind picture.

Purpose

To teach students to locate text language and details that help them create mind pictures

Materials and Preparation

Pre-read your read-aloud choice. Choose a part that paints a vivid mental picture for you. Identify the words and sentences that help you to create the picture. Copy that section onto chart paper.

2. STATE THE PURPOSE OF THE STRATEGY

Stephanie: Today, we are going to explore how an author's language and our mind pictures are connected. As I am reading Chapter 6, "Mr. Hiller," I want you to pay close attention to the mind pictures you are making. And I want you to listen for the language that Clyde Bulla uses that brings that picture to life.

3. MODEL THE STRATEGY

Stephanie reads Chapter 6. In it, Mr. Hiller, a man from the local nursery, talks to Gregory's class about plants. He draws the types of plants the students may want to grow in their own gardens. Gregory is excited about having a garden, but his mother reminds him that they do not have land for a garden. Gregory goes out to look at the burnt building behind his house. As Stephanie finishes, she puts down the book and thinks aloud.

Stephanie: I saw this chapter so vividly in my mind. Gregory stood in the burned building behind his house. He had a sad look on his face; his shoulders slumped slightly. He had a piece of chalk in his hand, and he stood facing a wall that had turned black from the fire's smoke. Now, let's think about how the pictures that we create while reading are directly connected to the words the author uses. While reading, I paid close attention to my mind pictures and the language that Clyde Bulla was using. I'd like to share the exact words that helped produce my mind picture.

4. EXPLORE A TEXT CLOSELY

Stephanie opens the book to a marked page. Then she shows the class the same text copied onto a chart: "He looked outside. There was concrete all around the house. He looked in the burned building. The floor there was concrete too. Mother was right. He had no place for a garden. He wanted to plant all the things Mr. Hiller had drawn on the blackboard. The curly lettuce was what he liked best. He took a piece of chalk and drew a bunch on the wall."

Stephanie: As I read this section, think about my mind picture. I saw Gregory looking sad, with a piece of chalk in his hands, facing a burnt wall. Let's see what words helped me paint that picture. *(Reads the passage, pauses, and gives the students time to think.)*

Stephanie: I pictured Gregory in the burnt building looking all around at the concrete and black walls, looking very sad. He knows he can't grow things so he is frowning and looking defeated. *(Points to the passage.)* This part here proves it: "The floor was concrete too. Mother was right. He had no place for a garden."

Xiao: I think your mind picture makes sense because Gregory is sad because he can't grow things, and he is in the burned building. You see the part where he draws lettuce on the wall? *(Stephanie points to the sentence.)* That part proves to me he is outside because that is where he draws.

Stephanie: Good point, Xiao. So, going back into the text really shows us where a mind picture comes from and that we understand what we read.

After a few days of pinpointing the language that creates a mind picture as a whole group, Stephanie asks students to try it on their own during readers respond. See page 89 for details.

5. SEND STUDENTS TO PRACTICE

Stephanie: Today, as you read independently, pay attention to language that helps create pictures in your mind. During reader's share, I'll ask a few of you to explain the part of the book that gave you the mind picture. While reading, you may want to mark parts you want to share with post-it notes.

MINI-LESSON

Deepen the Strategy

Capturing the Mind Picture that Lingers After Reading

1. MAKE A CONNECTION

Stephanie calls the class together to continue reading *The Chalk Box Kid*, but shares a concern first.

Stephanie: After I finished the last chapter of *The Chalk Box Kid*, I was a bit confused because I had so many pictures running through my head. I felt like I was flipping through a stack of photographs from a party and looking for the best one, the one I wanted to put in a frame. I wanted a picture that had most of the guests in it. Maybe a picture of blowing out candles or opening presents, the most memorable parts of the party. I want to have one clear picture that represents the chapter.

Purpose

To help students find the central meaning of a text by creating one composite image

Materials and Preparation

Pre-read a later chapter of your read-aloud choice.

That might mean pulling parts of a few different pictures to make one picture that represents my full understanding of the chapter.

2. STATE THE PURPOSE OF THE STRATEGY

Stephanie: Today we will focus on making one mind picture of the most important thing or things that happened in a chapter. This will help you understand what you read. You might just have to call up one picture or you might have to combine different pictures into one clear image.

3. READ ALOUD

Stephanie: I'm going to read the chapter straight through. But I'll pause to give you time to think about what's happening. I want you to focus on creating one picture. It can have details from different parts of the chapter. What are the important parts? You might want to pretend you're illustrating the chapter. Different readers might have different opinions about what's most important, which is okay. You just need to be able to explain the picture you remember and why it's important. Okay?

The students nod and prepare to listen. Stephanie reads Chapter 8. In it, Gregory's classmates follow him home and discover that the garden is drawn with chalk. Vance, who often bullies Gregory, claims the garden is nothing. Ivy is there, too. Every few pages, Stephanie pauses to allow the students to reflect and let their mind pictures take shape.

4. SHARE AS A WHOLE GROUP

Stephanie: Find the picture that best represents your understanding of this chapter. Belinda, would you like to start?

Belinda: I tried what you suggested. I closed my eyes and went through all the pictures I got in my head. The one that keeps coming up is Gregory standing near the wall where he has drawn the garden. He can hear Vance saying, "It's nothing" and laughing. Ivy is standing in the door of the burned-out building. I can see her head poking into the door.

Stephanie: Why does that image represent the most important part of this chapter as you understand it?

Belinda: In the chapter, it says that Ivy was the last one out of the building and that she almost stopped. I think it's important that she saw Gregory's pictures. I think that she wanted to stay, but was afraid of what the other kids would say.

Stephanie: I like how you described going through all your pictures and paying attention to the one that came up again and again. That is a good way of deciding which pieces of the chapter were most important to your comprehension. Can someone describe a different image? Joseph?

Joseph: The picture that stays in my mind is of Gregory lying in his bed at the end. He's all alone and that's why this is the most important picture. All his classmates left him, including Ivy, and then his mom thought he was bragging! I think Gregory feels sad and alone. He said that he doesn't care what his classmates think. I think he does.

Stephanie: Thanks, Joseph. That's a great picture and I like how you described why it is important to you. You made a picture that wasn't described in the chapter. Readers do that sometimes. The chapter ends with Gregory's conversation with his mom, but you thought about him lying in bed all alone. That image captures how you understood the chapter. Nice job. Can one other person share? Tatiana?

Tatiana: In my mind picture, Gregory is talking to his mom and seeing Vance's face laughing at him and Ivy peering in the door in his head.

Stephanie: So in your picture, Tatiana, you've used details from different parts of the chapter to almost make a collage or composite picture. The picture you'll remember is Gregory talking to his mom while he's thinking about Vance and Ivy.

After a few days of capturing a lingering mind picture in a whole group, Stephanie asks students to create pictures that best represent their understanding of the chapter.

5. SEND STUDENTS TO PRACTICE

Stephanie: We've talked about the clues a book gives you when it's a good place to stop. When you come to a good stopping place in your independent-reading book, pause and find that memorable image. Think about what's happening that makes you want to remember that picture.

6. CONFER WITH INDIVIDUAL STUDENTS

After independent reading, Stephanie has students share one memorable picture with a partner while she listens in and responds.

Stephanie: Hi Dario. Hi Belinda. Who is going to go first? Dario?

Dario: *(Nods. He is reading a nonfiction book,* Dinosaur Dinners.*)*

Stephanie: Great. Dario, can you begin by showing us where you paused to find the one image that represents your understanding of this book?

Dario: *(Flips through the first few pages and stops at an illustration of three carnivorous dinosaurs.)* After this page, the book talks about ways that dinosaurs defended themselves from the meat-eaters. So I keep a picture of Tyrannosaurus in my mind and put it into the rest of the pages. Like on the next page it talks about Gallimimus who was fast and ran away from the meat-eaters. I pictured T-Rex chasing Gallimimus.

Stephanie: So you kind of did what Tatiana talked about, using details from different parts of the text to make a synthesized picture. Belinda, what about you?

Belinda: *(Flips through the pages of* Alligator Baby *by Robert Munsch.)* I am having a hard time making mind pictures when the pictures are right on the page.

Stephanie: That is tricky, Belinda. Maybe Dario could read a few pages to you and you could try to make mind pictures as he reads. I bet other students are having a similar problem. Could you share later today so we can discuss different strategies for making mind pictures while reading a picture book?

Assessment and Documentation

Writing and sketching mind pictures reinforces what students see as they read. Students are more likely to get a fuller understanding of the central meaning of what they read. It's also an excellent way to assess students. By reviewing their documented responses, you can see how they use mind pictures to deepen their comprehension. Here are some ways our students respond on paper to making mind pictures.

Purpose

To explore the connection between descriptive language and making mind pictures

Materials and Preparation

Draw a sample sketch of a mind picture from your read aloud. Give students paper and colored pencils or pens to create their own mind pictures.

Stephanie's sample sketch of Gregory in the burned-out building.

Model the Activity: For several days, students express mind pictures orally during read aloud and independent reading. To reinforce the connection between text details and mind pictures, we create sketches. We start by choosing a passage from our read-aloud book that conjures up powerful images. As we talk about the picture the author's words make in our minds, we sketch it on a chart. (See sample above.) From there, students sketch their own mind pictures in notebooks, following read aloud.

Send Students to Practice: After several days of practicing as a group, we encourage students to try sketching mind pictures during independent reading.

Assess the Work: As we review sketches and conference with students about them, we keep these questions in mind:

- ⊚ Can this student visualize what he or she read?

- ⊚ Does this student pay attention to the images that come into his or her mind while reading?

Writing Sketch Captions

Katrina   6/10/   Fig Pudding

The mind image I got in my mind was when Cliff and Nate were in their bedroom sitting down and having memory about Brad. They were thinking of what Brad looked like because Nate couldnt remember what he looked like. Nate was crying because he felt bad that Brad died Nate ate his steaming bowl of Sadness. Cliff hasn't cryed so Cliff hasn't eaten his steaming bowl of Sadness. Cliff and Nate were talking in a low, soft and not that clear. Their dad came inside and said to Nate "It was Okay" Nate said It wasn't fair that Brad had died."

In her caption, Katrina demonstrates how she can go back into FIG PUDDING *and locate the words that created her mind picture.*

Model the Activity: As students become comfortable making sketches of their mind pictures, we ask them to provide captions for their sketches. We start by showing them a sketch we created, based on the read-aloud book. We then show an overhead of the passage that inspired the sketch. Together, we comb through the passage, looking for the phrases and sentences that created the picture.

We add the phrases and sentences to the sketch as a caption. From there, we ask students to find captions for their read-aloud sketches.

Send Students to Practice: After a few days of pinpointing and writing captions as a group, we ask students to try it on their own, on the sketches they create in independent reading. (See sample above.)

Assess the Work: Having students add a caption to a sketch is a wonderful way to assess their ability to recognize details as they read. While conferring with students over their sketches and captions, we ask ourselves:

- Is this student paying attention to the images that come to mind as he or she reads?

- Can this student pinpoint the language that creates the mind picture?

Purpose

To urge students to find the words in the text that create the mind picture, and use them as a caption for the sketch

Materials and Preparation

Post a sketch based on a passage from your read-aloud book. Create an overhead transparency of pages that inspired the sketch.

Purpose

To have students compile their composite mind pictures into a picture book that tells a complete story

Materials and Preparation

Gather and distribute paper and colored pens and pencils

Creating Illustrated Books from Chapter Books

Model the Activity: After spending several days discussing and sharing composite mind pictures—pictures that represent the most memorable section of a text—we have students create an illustrated book based on our read-aloud book. Students choose or are assigned different chapters and create mind pictures that represent those chapters. (They usually need to re-read the chapters.) The students then write descriptions of the scenes, explaining why their pictures represent the most important or memorable moment.

Send Students to Practice: After a few days of creating composite sketches as a group, students create picture books or comic books from chapter books, in small groups or alone. (See sample below.)

Assess the Work: While reviewing the picture and comic books, and conferring with the students who created them, we ask ourselves:

- Can this student visualize what he or she read?

- Is this student paying attention to the images that come to mind as he or she reads?

- Can this student pinpoint the language that creates the mind picture?

- Can this student synthesize small pictures into a composite picture to understand the text's central meaning?

A page from Ozzie's comic book.

Closing Thoughts

Our study lasts about four weeks. Once most students are using the strategy independently, we know it's time to move on. Making mind pictures becomes another tool in the students' repertoire of reading strategies.

CHAPTER 8

Identifying the Big Ideas

How many times have your students retold an entire story when all you asked them for was the big idea? Young readers often get bogged down in details and lose the author's central message. When proficient readers read, they distinguish key ideas from details, and come away with a clear understanding of that message. Our students call that message "the big idea." And when they are able to identify it, the text has greater impact and is more likely to stay with them.

Identifying the big idea requires synthesizing information and drawing conclusions. Students can be taught these skills through thoughtful modeling, purposeful teaching, clear examples, supportive small-group work, one-to-one conferring, and plenty of time for practice.

OVERVIEW
of the Study

We teach identifying a text's big idea in three phases, guiding students toward practicing the strategy independently. Specifically, we:

- introduce the strategy, teaching students to determine the most important idea in sections of text.

- extend the strategy, teaching students to check their comprehension by finding the evidence that supports the big idea.

- deepen the strategy, teaching students that the big ideas in sections are clues to the book's central message.

We start by helping students understand the definition of a big idea. Then we help them to read in chunks to identify the big idea. Finally we teach them to look for the central meaning of the entire text. This process takes time, but can be done if it's broken down into manageable steps that students can understand.

Choosing a Read-Aloud Text to Teach Identifying the Big Ideas

We look for either a fiction or nonfiction book that contains clear, central ideas supported by strong details. The book should contain text features that support students in drawing conclusions. For example, chapter titles that give a clue to the chapter's meaning, supporting pictures, and predictable story lines.

For this study, we chose the narrative nonfiction book *Chasing the Moon to China* by Virginia Overton McLean, which is about a girl who travels to China with her family. In it, the girl documents what she is learning and wondering through photographs and drawings. At the end of the book, when she is leaving China, the girl realizes that her trip has sparked her interest in the world. She has gained so much knowledge, but realizes that there is still more to learn. Each two-page spread in the book covers a single topic, with supporting illustrations, photos, and details.

Great Books for Identifying the Big Ideas

My Name Is Maria Isabel
by Alma Flora Ada
(Aladdin)

Food and Festivals series
(Steck-Vaughn)

Fig Pudding
by Ralph Fletcher
(Clarion Books)

Chasing the Moon to China
by Virginia Overton McLean (Redbird Press)

MINI-LESSON

Introduce the Strategy
Distinguishing the Big Ideas

1. INTRODUCE THE LESSON

Stephanie calls the class together.

Stephanie: I am so excited because I found a truly amazing book about a little girl who travels to China for the first time. As we read, we will learn about China along with her. *(Flips through the book and reads the first page. The students determine the book is nonfiction, but written in a narrative voice. They also notice that the book has photographs, but no chapters or headings.)*

2. STATE THE PURPOSE OF THE STRATEGY

Stephanie: We'll learn a lot of important details about China. Details help us make mind pictures, bring the setting to life, help us understand characters, and make us want to keep reading. They also help us to pay attention to the author's most important idea—"the big idea."

Anna: Are big ideas like morals in fables?

Stephanie: In a way, but big ideas can be found in any text, fiction or nonfiction. Deciding what the big idea is and what details are can be confusing at times. It is helpful to pause and ask yourself, "What was the most important thing I just learned?" Today, we are going try to determine the big idea as we read *Chasing the Moon to China*. As I read the first five pages, I want you to listen for what you think is the most important information. When I stop reading, we will talk about what we think is the big idea and what we think are details.

3. MODEL THE STRATEGY

Stephanie reads the first five pages. When she is done, she shows an overhead transparency of page two.

Stephanie: Before I started reading, you noticed that this book is not broken up by chapters or headings. Instead, every two pages, there are new photos and a drawing. So, to help us understand Virginia's big ideas, we are going to look at her story in two-page chunks. Today, we'll determine Virginia's big idea and details on pages two and three. *(Points to the overhead and holds up the book to show students the corresponding pages.)*

Purpose

To show students how to read for the most important idea to understand an author's main message

Materials and Preparation

Pre-read your read-aloud choice. Make an overhead transparency of two facing pages that clearly display details and a central idea. Have post-it notes on hand to jot down the big ideas.

Stephanie: Here, Virginia tells us that her family can't stop talking about what they already know about China. They eat Chinese food and read Chinese folktales. She learns how important and wonderful dragons are in Chinese culture. She says dragons are like imaginative angels in the sky searching out knowledge. These are details that bring the story to life. *(Replaces the overhead of page 2 with page 3.)*

Stephanie: Here, her father talks about China's history and her mom talks about its population. These points are important because they help us see that her family is excited, but I don't think that they are the big idea. They help us understand the characters better, but aren't what the entire book is about. Look at this passage here:

"But I kept wondering what China would really be like. How would the people look? What kind of houses would they live in? Would the Chinese children look like me? How would China smell? How would it sound?"

I think the big idea is that Virginia is wondering what China will be like.

4. SHARE AS A WHOLE GROUP

Stephanie: What are you thinking about the big idea and the details?

Tahiris: I think that the big idea is that Virginia wants to know what China will be like because this is her story. Plus, the words that you read to us are below her picture and her picture is on the page before.

Jayvon: I think it is that she is excited. The whole page talks about it. Going on a trip is exciting. She also learns about a dragon, and that is exciting. That is definitely the big idea.

Anna: I'm not so sure I agree. The dragon is a cool part, but I think it's a detail. I think the author put it in to make us to want to read more. Like in *Nate the Great* stories, there are letters and you always know it's a clue and you want to read on to solve it. I think the big idea is about her wonderings. When we flipped through the book we saw pictures of houses, kids, and what China looks like! I wonder about those things too.

Stephanie is aware that Tahiris simply repeated what she said, that Jayvon is drawn to exciting details, and that Anna needs to be challenged. This information is important to planning how she will teach the strategy.

Stephanie: Right, details are like clues. They point us to the big idea. Our job is to weed through the details and figure out what is most important and what will help us as we read. Let's make a note that Virginia is wondering what China will be like. *(Writes on a post-it note that Virginia is curious about what Chinese people look like and how they live, about the smells and sounds of China, and places it in the book.)*

5. SEND STUDENTS TO PRACTICE

Stephanie: As you read independently today, pay attention to the details the author uses to bring the story alive. You may want to pause after reading a few pages and try to write the big idea on a post-it note. I will check in with you to see how it is going. *(Students disperse around the classroom and get started with independent reading.)*

6. CONFER WITH INDIVIDUAL STUDENTS

Stephanie sits down next to Jayvon because she noted during the lesson that he may need help distinguishing the big idea from a detail.

Stephanie: Jayvon, how is it going?

Jayvon: I'm okay. I am reading *Pinky and Rex and the Spelling Bee.*

Stephanie: That's the perfect book to try out finding the big idea. How about we work on that strategy together?

Jayvon: Yeah, that sounds good.

Stephanie: Perfect. Can you tell me a little bit about the book?

Jayvon: Well, I've read one chapter. Pinky and Rex are walking to school, and Pinky is excited because there is a spelling test and he has been getting ready all week. He's a good speller. Rex forgot about the test and she gets so sad. She sits down on the sidewalk. She wants to go home and tell her mom that she is sick. Pinky says that she can't do that. Rex is sad because she is a bad speller and the whole class will laugh. Pinky says that he won't laugh at her and that she is really smart at other things like games and dinosaurs and stuff. She says she doesn't care, and that she is moving to the moon if they laugh at her.

Stephanie: Wow! You kept track of a lot of details, and details can help you figure out the big idea. They are your clues. What are most of the details about?

Jayvon: The spelling test that is going to happen and Rex.

Stephanie: Great. Think about the details as clues. What did you learn about Rex and the spelling test?

Jayvon: Rex is scared to take the spelling test because she is afraid the class will laugh at her because she can't spell.

Stephanie: That's right! That's what is most important. That's the big idea. You did a great job. Why don't you go ahead and read the next chapter. Stop at the end and think about what was most important, and jot down your thought on a post-it note. I will check in with you at the end of reading workshop and see how it is going.

Extend the Strategy
Finding Evidence for the Big Idea

Purpose

To check comprehension by finding the details that support the big idea

Materials and Preparation

Pre-read your read-aloud choice. Have a chart ready to record the big idea and evidence that supports it.

1. MAKE A CONNECTION

Stephanie calls the class together.

Stephanie: We are learning so much from *Chasing the Moon to China*, many details and big ideas.

2. STATE THE PURPOSE OF THE STRATEGY

Stephanie: Today, we are going to work on supporting our big ideas with evidence from the book by summarizing. Summarizing is restating the big idea in your own words. Details provide evidence for summaries.

3. MODEL THE STRATEGY

Stephanie reads two pages of *Chasing the Moon to China*. When she is done, she thinks aloud.

Stephanie: Wow! What an interesting part. They plow their fields without a tractor. Most families wash dishes by hand, wash clothes in a river or a small tin basin, and do not have a refrigerator. I'd say that the big idea is that, in many parts of China, people do a lot by hand because they don't have a lot of machines, like we do here. All the details talk about that.

Winnie: What about the part where people are pulling wood in carts instead of a car, like we do? They were also pulling a refrigerator on a cart.

Stephanie: Virginia did state that. Let's go back and reread to help us understand. We can see if the point you are making is a detail or the most important thing. *(Rereads the text.)*

Winnie: Oh, I get it! My thought is just a detail that shows people do things by hand.

Stephanie: It's also evidence for the big idea that people in China do a lot of things by hand. *(Adds the big idea and details to a T-chart. [See sample right.])*

4. PAIR UP STUDENTS

Stephanie: Now, I am going to read two more pages. When I am done, you are going to turn and talk with a partner about what you think the big idea is and why. I will show the pages on the overhead so that you can reread if you need to. *(Reads the next two pages, turns on the overhead, and gives the students a few minutes to share their thoughts with a partner.)*

5. CONFER WITH PARTNERS

Stephanie circulates and listens in on the conversations to assess their understanding of the strategy. She sits down next to Anthony and Lavert.

Stephanie: So, how is it going?

Lavert: Okay. I think that the big idea is that people in China have different food than we do. We eat at fast-food places like McDonalds. They don't. *(Stephanie notes that Lavert pointed out a single detail. She plans to follow up in a conference and guided reading.)*

Anthony: Well, I think the big idea is that they have different food stores. They shop for food alongside the road from vendors, and they buy meat from a stall where meat hangs from hooks above their heads. We learned before that there aren't many refrigerators.

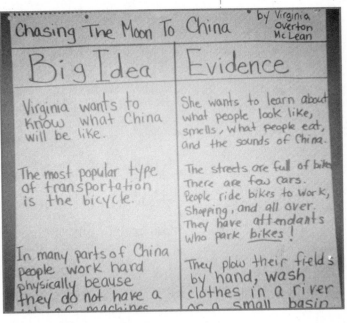

Stephanie charts each two-page spread's big idea and evidence that proves the idea.

Lavert: There are more details on that than on what I thought. That is the big idea. It is more important.

Stephanie: Good points. I think you two are learning a lot from each other. Sometimes it helps to go back into the book to see if you can find the details to support what you are thinking. Thanks for showing us that, Anthony. You two may want to share your strategy with the class.

After a few days of identifying big ideas as a group, Stephanie asks students to record big ideas and evidence from their independent-reading books on T-charts. See page 101 for details.

MINI-LESSON

Deepen the Strategy
Discovering a Whole Book's Big Idea

Purpose

To determine a book's central message by keeping track of big ideas while reading

Materials and Preparation

Read and finish the last three pages of your read-aloud choice. Post the big idea chart.

1. MAKE A CONNECTION

Stephanie calls the class together.

Stephanie: I was looking over our chart this morning, and I noticed we have learned a lot about China through Virginia's experiences. We have learned about transportation, food, homes, recreational activities, religion, national monuments, art, family life, children, and school.

2. STATE THE PURPOSE OF THE STRATEGY

Stephanie: We're going to finish the book today, and note the big idea for the final pages. Then we'll look back at our chart of big ideas to see if we can understand the big idea for the entire book. Good readers ask themselves, "Why did the author write this? What does she want me to learn?" *(Reads the next three pages of* Chasing The Moon To China. *Virginia begins to notice that she is also like children in China. They go on field trips to the zoo, eat ice cream, play musical instruments, watch parades, love fireworks, and have similar wonderings about the world. When it is time to leave, she is sad, but curious to learn more about China.)*

3. MODEL THE STRATEGY

Stephanie: Wow! What a powerful way to end the book. I really loved it. First, let's talk about the big idea of these pages. *(Discusses the big idea with* *students: Virginia sees similarities between herself and Chinese children. Stephanie notes the big idea on the chart, as she did in the previous min-lesson.)* Now, when I look back at the last page, we are given insight about what Virginia is thinking. Listen to the last page again:

"I had seen how I was like the Chinese people and how I was different; yet I was almost as curious as when I'd come. I wanted to know and understand more, but perhaps that is learning. Like the ancient dragon, I was chasing the moon, the pearl of wisdom."

I think that this gives us a clue to the entire book's big idea. Authors often do that, end their stories giving you something to think about. Here, we are getting personal with Virginia again. It's like she's giving us a message. How can we dig deeper to find out what her message, or big idea, is?

Lavert: What I am doing is reading the chart. Look at the first big idea.

Stephanie: Good point, Lavert. Let's go back and see what big ideas we kept track of as we read. *(Points to the chart and reads aloud.)* The first thing we wrote is:

"Virginia is wondering what China is like. She is specifically curious about what Chinese people look like, how they live, what the smells and sounds of China are."

Let's continue to read the rest of the big ideas on the chart.

4. SHARE AS A WHOLE GROUP

Stephanie and the students finishing reading the chart.

Stephanie: Now that we have read all the big ideas, what do you think they are telling us?

Katrina: Most of the big ideas we wrote are about the things that Virginia learned. And about differences between her and Chinese people, and then, at the end, how they are alike.

Stephanie: True, she did tell us about the things she learned while in China. The first big idea we noted was Virginia's questions.

Winnie: Then she finds the answers to her questions while she is in China. The last big idea is that she has more questions because she learned about all the things she wondered about before she left.

Anthony: I think her trip taught her that when you learn something, it makes you excited and you want to learn more. All her big ideas along the way show us that she is learning.

Stephanie: Yes, I think you're right. Her big message is that learning about another culture is fun and it never ends. Learning about similarities and differences is only the beginning. By getting to know the people and culture, you only want to learn more!

5. SEND STUDENTS TO PRACTICE

Stephanie: Today, as you read independently, read with the author's purpose in mind. You may want to ask yourself, "Why did the author write this? What does she want me to learn?" Then, at the end of independent reading, see if you can figure out the author's big idea for the whole book.

After a few days of talking about a book's big idea as a group, Stephanie asks students to try it on their own by creating tables of contents for their independent-reading books. See page 102 for details.

Assessment and Documentation

Writing and drawing are wonderful ways to reinforce students' comprehension as they read. They can also help students to find a book's big ideas and clarify an author's message. So, in addition to providing a lot of modeling and support during our study, we give students opportunities to document their responses in writing and drawing during independent reading.

These responses provide us with windows into students' understanding of the strategy. They demonstrate how well students are progressing throughout the study. This information is extremely valuable in tailoring our lessons to meet our students' needs. Here are some of the ways we gather responses during our study on identifying the big idea.

The Big Idea T-Chart

Record Information as a Class: While we read *Chasing the Moon to China* to the students, we record the big ideas and the details that support them on a T-chart. This provides use with a permanent record of the book's big ideas, which we can refer back to as necessary.

Send Students to Practice: We model filling out the T-chart for a few days before asking students to do so independently. During readers respond, students record the big ideas from their independent-reading books, on photocopied T-charts or in their notebooks, using the class T-chart as a model. (See sample above.)

As students become more proficient at this, we suggest they record big ideas as they read. We must be careful about this, though, because some children's comprehension breaks down if they stop reading to write.

Assess the Work: As we read over individual T-charts and conference with students about their big ideas, we keep these questions in mind:

- Can this student distinguish the big idea from details?
- Can this student find evidence to support the big idea?

Name: McKenzie   Date: 3/7

Big Idea T-Chart

Title: Post Cards From China   Author: Zoé Dawson

Big Idea	Details That Support It
The big idea is that an army made out of clay is where the Emperor is buried	- That the emperor was buried with the soldiers. - The clay is called terra-cotta.
The big idea is that Boats carry goods down the Chang river	- boats carry goods - boats carry people - The Chang river is the longest river in China

Mckenzie charts big ideas and supporting evidence from POSTCARDS FROM CHINA.

Purpose

To record big ideas and details as students read

Materials and Preparation

Prepare a large T-chart on chart paper. Write "Big Idea" at the top of the left-hand column and "Details that Support the Big Idea" at the top of the right-hand column. Photocopy enough blank T-charts for each student. (See Appendix 10.) Or students can make their own in their notebooks.

Purpose

To keep track of big ideas while reading and to create a table of contents for the book based on them

Materials and Preparation

Post blank chart paper and your finished class T-chart with big ideas from your read-aloud book. Be sure students have their finished individual T-charts and blank paper.

Table of Contents

Model the Activity:

From our class big-idea T-chart, we make a table of contents for *Chasing the Moon to China.* We start by reminding students that each title in a table of contents needs to reflect the most important message in that section, the big idea. We then reread the big ideas and details on our class T-chart. From there, we write a title for each big idea that clearly states what a reader will find.

Send Students to Practice: After creating a table of contents as a class, we ask students to create them on their own,

based on the individual T-charts they created for their independent-reading books. (See sample above.)

1. Excited News
2. Nerdy Nephew
3. Meeting Too-Tall And His Gang
4. No Luck At All
5. Being Mr. Know It All
6. Talking About Ferdy
7. Liking Queenie
8. A Show
9. Playing And Getting Hurt
10. Getting Lost!
11. Being Sorry
12. Being Happy

1. I pick Excited news because Brother's and Sister's uncle was going to come and bring a surprise for him.
2. I pick Nerdy Nephew because sister and Brother's surprise was there nephew Ferdy. He was a nerdy nephew because he was bossy.
3. I picked Meeting Too-Tall because Ferdy meets Tootall and they started yelling at each other.
4. I picked No Luck At All because Brother had to get stuck with Ferdy in his class. He was unlucky.
5. I pick Being Mr. Not so Much because Ferdy thought he was Mr. Not So Much by answering every question.
6. I pick Talking About Ferdy because Brother was talking about how much Brother Knows.
7. I pick liking Queenie because Ferdy likes Queenie a lot.
8. I pick A show because Ferdy does a show about science.
9. I pick playing and getting Hurt because Ferdy plays with Too-Tall and gets hurt.
10. I pick getting lost because Ferdy gets lost in the woods.
11. I pick Being sorry because Brother feels sorry about Ferdy being in trouble.
12. I pick Being happy because Ferdy was happy because he was going to be playing football.

Katrina's table of contents

Assess the Work: Making a table of contents is a wonderful way to assess students' ability to synthesize information. Students also have to draw upon what they know about how books are organized. While reviewing the work and conferring with students, we ask ourselves:

- ◎ Can this student synthesize small pieces of information?
- ◎ Can this student draw conclusions?

Letter to the Author

Model the Activity: When students finish a book, they often have questions, opinions, and thoughts. Letter writing provides a forum for them to react to the book. By voicing their feelings in writing, students gain deeper understanding of the book's central meaning.

We model letter writing on chart paper during read aloud, discussing what a good letter contains. We show students how to express an opinion about a big idea and use details from the story to support that opinion.

Send Students to Practice:

After a few days modeling letter writing, we ask students to write their own letters to the author of their independent-reading book.

Assess the Work:

Letter writing is an excellent way to measure a student's depth of understanding of an author's message. While reading individual letters and conferring with students, we ask ourselves:

- ◎ Can this student synthesize small pieces of information?

- ◎ Can this student draw conclusions?

- ◎ Can this student identify the book's central meaning?

> April 27
>
> Dear Virginia,
>
> We are writing to thank you for writing your book *Chasing the Moon to China*. Our class just began a study of the communities and cultures of China. We truly enjoyed your book, and we learned so much by reading it.
>
> When we first began our study of China we made a list of things we wanted to learn. We were excited to know that what we wanted to learn about, you also wanted to learn about. We too want to learn what China is really like, what do their homes look like, what foods do they eat, what is their major form of transportation what are the sounds, smells and children like? Thank you for sharing all your information and pictures about these topics. We found it so interesting that people bike everywhere. We wish that more people would do that in New York. We hope that people now have more machines to help them with their work. Plowing a field by hand, or pulling a refrigerator with a bike just seems like really hard work. We were also excited to learn that kids go to school just like us. The way they write is so beautiful.
>
> Your book taught us that China is a beautiful place with so many interesting things to learn. We realize now that there is so much to learn about China, that our inquiry is just the beginning and we will never be able to learn it all. "Chasing the Moon to China"— searching for knowledge— is going to be an exciting adventure. Maybe you can join us on our journey by writing back to us and sharing other things you have learned about China.
>
> Respectfully,
> Ms. Yulga and Class 3-1

Stephanie and her class wrote this letter to Virginia Overton in response to the big ideas they got from her book. This letter serves as a model for children when they write letters independently.

Purpose

To have students share their thoughts and opinions about the book's central message by writing a letter to the author

Materials and Preparation

Post blank chart paper and your finished class T-chart with big ideas from your read-aloud book. Be sure students have their finished individual T-charts and blank paper.

Closing Thoughts

Some students catch onto finding the big idea faster than others. Some are more comfortable finding them in nonfiction than in fiction. The amount of time you put into studying the strategy depends largely on the needs of your students. Once most students are using the strategy independently, it is time to move on and continue to support readers who struggle in guided reading and reading conferences.

Book Groups

Benefits of Book Groups

They allow students to:

- *ask clarifying questions and build on one another's thinking to arrive at a fuller understanding of the text.*

- *talk about what was going on in their minds as they read.*

- *use all the strategies in an authentic context.*

Although we teach comprehension strategies one by one to familiarize students with each of them, we know that good readers don't use them that way. Good readers use them seamlessly and subconsciously. When we finish studying a strategy, we tell students to continue using it along with the new strategies they're learning. However, they rarely do so on their own. So, we have them form book groups, which provide a supportive context for using all strategies simultaneously.

Book groups are usually made up of two to six students. (We have found smaller groups work better in the early grades). We set aside three 20-minute blocks each week for groups to meet. During those times, members decide on practical matters such as what book to read, when they will meet next, and how they will prepare. At the heart of book group, though, is the discussion about the text. Readers share their connections, predictions, mind pictures, questions, thoughts about the big idea, and overall impressions of the book. Often impressions about a book change or grow in complexity as students listen and respond to each other.

OVERVIEW
of Book Groups

Members follow a predictable cycle of planning for reading, reading independently, and discussing the reading. We teach students how to do each of these activities before expecting to work independently in groups.

- First, groups plan for reading. They must figure out what and how much they will read for the next meeting, make sure all group members do the required reading, and determine ways to ensure that each member will participate in the discussion.

- Next, students read independently, following the agreed-upon plan.

- Finally, students meet to discuss their reading, share their thinking, and deepen their comprehension. At the end of the meeting, groups reflect on and adjust their reading plans.

Forming Groups and Choosing Books

Before we begin book groups, we select a variety of books for students to choose from. In the early grades, we form the groups and then give members two or three books to choose from that we know they can read with little support. We usually stick to realistic fiction because we've found that students comprehend it more easily than other genres. Sometimes we choose first books in series so that students get the support of the group in getting to know characters, setting, text structure, and so forth. From there, students can read other books in the series independently, with greater ease.

With older children, we introduce five or six books to the whole class and ask students to choose three that interest them. Then we form the groups based primarily on interest, taking into account reading level and chemistry among members.

Good Series for 2nd- to 4th-Grade Book Groups

Secrets of Droon by Tony Abbott (Scholastic)

Amber Brown by Paula Danzinger (Putnam)

Kids of Polk Street School by Patricia Reilly Giff (Doubleday)

The Zack Files by Dan Greenburg (Grosset & Dunlap)

Magic Tree House by Mary Pope Osborne (Random House)

Junie B. Jones by Barbara Park (Random House)

American Girls by various authors (Pleasant Company)

Bullseye Step into Classics by various authors (Random House)

Introducing Book Groups
Planning for Reading

Purpose

To work collaboratively to determine how the group will function

Materials and Preparation

Before this lesson, groups should be formed and books selected. Allow three 20-minute blocks of time each week for groups to meet. Each child will need a copy of the book. Prepare a "What to Do During Book Groups" chart to display in the classroom. (See page 107.) Make enough photocopies of the "Book Group Plan" (Appendix 11) and "Response Sheet" (Appendix 12) for each student.

1. MAKE A CONNECTION

Nicole calls the class together.

Nicole: Each of you is now part of a book group and each group has decided on a book it wants to read. Are any of your parents in book groups?

Kristen: My aunt is. A few weeks ago she had her group over to her house to talk about the book they were reading.

Nicole: I'm in a book group, too. Lots of adults are. So what you are going to do in your book groups is something that good readers do. They choose a book they want to read, read it independently, and then meet to talk about it.

STATE THE PURPOSE OF BOOK GROUPS

Nicole: In book groups, you will read like adults. Adult readers use lots of strategies as they read, just like you do. But they use strategies all at once instead of focusing on mind pictures or connections or predictions. They call up whatever strategy will help them understand. So be sure to keep track of the strategies you use. You will meet in groups on Mondays, Wednesdays, and Fridays to talk about your reading.

3. DISCUSS PLANNING AS A WHOLE GROUP

Nicole: Before you read, though, groups have to plan. What do you think groups should plan before they read?

Morgan: They should decide how much to read so people don't get ahead of each other.

Nicole: That's very important. Book groups need to plan how much they will read before the next group meeting. I've made a chart of the things groups must plan, and that's first on the list. *(See sample page 107.)*

Before we introduce book groups, we practice this kind of decision making in guided reading. We ask, "What strategies might be helpful as we read this text?" "How many paragraphs should we read before we talk about what we are thinking?" This prepares students to work in groups, independent of the teacher.

Nicole: At the first book-group meeting, you need to decide on these things:

⊚ How much will you read between meetings?
⊚ How will you document the strategies you use?
⊚ How will you hold each other accountable for doing the assigned reading?
⊚ How will you ensure that each member of the group participates in the discussion?

Dylan: What do you mean, "document the strategies you use"?

Nicole: That's a great question. What do you think? How could you document the strategies you use?

Taylor: We could use post-its to write down the strategies we use.

Nicole: Great suggestion. Anything else?

Lauren: We could write them down in our reading notebooks.

Nicole: You could do that, too. I thought that might be difficult. So I want to give you the option of using a response sheet as you read. (*Shows the response sheet.*) As you plan in your groups, I'll explain the sheet so you can decide if you want to use it, post-its, or your reading notebooks. (*Distributes the planning sheets so that students know exactly what's expected.*)

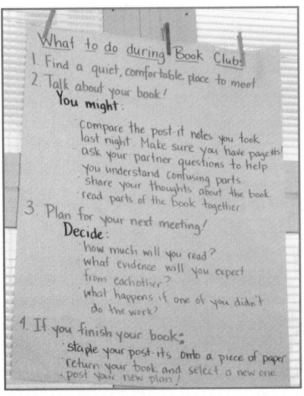

Nicole hangs this chart in her classroom so readers can refer to it in book groups.

⊚

Good Series for 4th- and 5th-Grade Book Groups

The Time Warp Trio by Jon Scieska (Viking)

Dear America by various authors (Scholastic)

My Name Is America by various authors (Scholastic)

The Childhood of Famous Americans by various authors (Aladdin)

The Royal Diary by various authors (Scholastic)

4. Send Students to Plan for Reading

Nicole: Now, you will meet in your groups and plan how you will go about reading your book. Each group member should have a copy of the planning sheet.

Students move to various sections of the room to meet in groups. As students discuss their plans, Nicole moves from group to group, listening in and giving suggestions. She shows the response sheet so groups can decide whether they want to use it to document their reading.

5. Make Plans Public

Once plans are made, we ask students to post them. We find that students take their plans more seriously when they are available for everyone to see.

Taylor, Caroline, Kostas, and Aidan plan their discussion. They will read two chapters before each meeting, use a coding sheet to document questions and thoughts, and assign jobs such as sketching mind pictures and looking for new vocabulary words.

Name: Taylor   Date: 10-4

Book Group Plan

Group Members: Taylor, Caroline, Kostas, Aidan

Author: Guns for General Washington Seymour Reit

Your group will meet every other day. What will members expect of one another? To have read enough and to explain what happened.

How many pages will each member read between meetings? 2 chapters

What sort of documentation should members bring to the group? Questions and thoughts on a coding sheet of paper.

What happens if a member comes unprepared? Do their work at recess.

How will you conduct your discussion? Each member needs to be involved. We will have jobs.

At the end of the meeting, each member should write a brief reflection on how talking about the book changed his or her understanding of the book.

Preparing for Book Groups
Reading Independently

1. STATE THE PURPOSE OF INDEPENDENT READING

Before independent reading, Nicole conducts a brief whole-group meeting.

Nicole: Today in independent reading, you will read your book-group book. You do not have to read that book every day in independent reading. Just today. That way, if you have difficulty understanding your book or following your plan, I can help you.

2. SEND STUDENTS TO READ INDEPENDENTLY

Nicole: Before you begin reading, check over your plan to make sure you know how much to read and how you will document your thinking as you read.

3. CONFER WITH INDIVIDUAL STUDENTS

During independent reading, Nicole circulates around the room, making sure that students are following their plans and recording their thinking. (See sample below.) In conferences, she typically asks students:

- Can you explain your group's plan in your own words?
- What strategies are working for you as you read?
- Are there any places in the text where you had a hard time comprehending?
- How are you recording what you are thinking about as you read?

Purpose

To read independently, after groups have made their plans

Materials and Preparation

Make sure students have their book, plan, and response sheet, post-its, or reading notebook to document their reading.

Page(s)	What's happening while you read? (Code)	Please write your thoughts here...
50	?D	Who is singing?
52	?D	Will they make it back to Cambrige?
53	V	Word: Yoked :. Definition: paired are attached to a cart.
62	?D	Will old Toby catch a fish?
C.14	?A	What is "Dangerous Ice" about?
100	O	I just had ring mind picture of the sled creaking and then collapsing
104	V	Word: dispatch Definition: a message sent with speed

Taylor's coding sheet, which was made specifically for historical fiction by Nicole's colleague Meghan Grassl.

?D = question during reading

?V = unknown vocabulary

?A = question after reading

O = other strategy

109

4. SHARE AS A WHOLE GROUP

After independent reading, Nicole calls the group back together.

Nicole: How did your reading go today? Were you able to follow the plan? Does anyone have any questions to ask the group?

Caroline: Things went well today. I like the response sheet. It's easy to record the different strategies I use. The one problem was that my group decided to read one chapter before each meeting, and I didn't quite finish.

Colin: I had the same problem.

Nicole: What do you think you can do?

Caroline: I was thinking that I could read this book at home tonight or during independent reading tomorrow because our book group doesn't meet until Wednesday.

Nicole: That sounds like a great plan. Keep in mind that you meet on Monday, Wednesday, and Friday, so you have independent reading in school and time at home to do the reading you need to do.

MINI-LESSON

Reflecting on Book Groups
Group Discussion

Purpose

To urge students to discuss how they are using all strategies to understand the text

1. STATE THE PURPOSE OF GROUP DISCUSSION

Nicole gathers her class before they will meet in their book groups.

Nicole: Today, you will meet in your book groups to discuss your reading. Can anyone look at our schedule and see what book groups replaces?

Aidan: I see that we are not having readers respond today.

Nicole: That's right. Instead we're meeting in book groups because talking about books is a way of responding to books. Instead of responding in writing, you're responding by speaking. You will have a discussion in response to your reading. Therefore, it's important to talk about your ideas, respond to each other's ideas. Group members might disagree about a prediction, agree about connections, or discuss possible answers to a question.

2. SEND STUDENTS INTO GROUP DISCUSSIONS

Nicole: You have twenty minutes for your group discussion. Spend the first fifteen minutes talking about the book. Spend the last five minutes reflecting on your plan. Is it working? Are there any changes that need to be made? I'll let you know when fifteen minutes has passed.

Students move into group discussions. They share their connections, predictions, mind pictures, questions, thoughts about the big idea, and overall impressions of the book. Depending on their plans, in some groups, members take turns sharing all their thoughts at once. In others, they share thoughts on one strategy at a time. We want readers to feel comfortable sharing passages where their comprehension breaks down. So, we encourage students to share those passages with the group. That way, members can decide together on the meaning.

3. ENCOURAGE REFLECTION

After fifteen minutes, Nicole calls for the whole group's attention.

Nicole: Okay, it's been fifteen minutes. Now you need to talk about how your plan is working. Think about the following questions:

Should you read more or less for the next meeting?

Do you need to change anything about the way you are documenting your thinking?

If everyone didn't have a chance to share, what changes can you make to your plan to make sure everyone does the next time?

Groups make the necessary adjustments to their plans.

Eryka and Jessica share notes they took as they read independently.

Assessment and Documentation

Assessment

During Independent reading: As students read independently, we ask them to talk about their groups' plans to make sure they understand what to do. We ask them to talk about the strategies they are using and whether there are places in the text that are difficult to comprehend. We record notes on these conferences as we do for any other reading conferences.

25	? D	Why would Paul want to fight in the A.M. Rev.?
33	? D	Will the war conncili accept Henry's plan?
38	? D	Will anyone get sick on the trip?
38	? D	Will they get caught in a blizzard?
46	? D	Will one of the people that went overboard get hypethermia?

Recording Sheet: This child is relying on asking questions while he reads. He needs to push himself to use other strategies.

During group discussion: When we listen in on discussions, we note whether students ask follow-up questions of one another. We note whether they are talking deeply or merely reading through their response lists. We note whether they isolate difficult spots. Often groups claim to be "finished" after only a few minutes. And usually, they have not responded to the thoughts members shared. We remind students that this is a conversation. Therefore, they should discuss, not simply report.

Reading Book Group

My thinking changed because my book group was talking about John and Mrs. Washington, I was thinking about the soliders and Mr. Washington. My reading thoughts also grew because my book group gave me good ideas.
90/26/01
My thinking changed because my group was talking about Perrie and I was thinking about Mrs. Washington and John.
10/29/01
My thinking changed on something else. I was thinking of Azor and Elisibiths coat but now I'm thinking of who was in the t and why?
10/31/01 My thinking changed because I was thinking of Azor and Elisibeths coat but now thinking of Oliver.

Group Thought Response: This child has a clear sense of how his thinking changed, from the very first meeting.

Documentation

Recording Sheets: The recording sheets are an excellent documentation tool. As we review them, we note what strategies each student is using. (See sample on page 112.) We also note whether strategy uses change over time. Do readers employ more strategies as they get further into the book or do they continue to use the same ones?

Recording sheets are also an excellent self-assessment tool. We ask students themselves to look at the strategies they are using. Students can immediately see whether they are using a variety of strategies or relying on only a couple. This helps them to monitor themselves, which builds independence.

Group Thought Responses: Occasionally, we ask students to write a brief response after their meeting. In it, they talk about how their thinking changed as a result of the discussion. If a student's thinking didn't change, we need to conference with that child to see what's going on. Perhaps the child isn't participating in the discussion and, therefore, his thinking remains static. The child might also be having trouble making meaning from the book. In that case, he might need to change his group or book, or work harder to use comprehension strategies.

Book Group Letters: After groups finish their books, we ask each member to write a letter to a fellow member, discussing his or her comprehension of the book and asking questions as necessary. (See sample right.) These letters reflect the kind of conversation that took place in the group and provide a lasting document of the experience. They can also shed light on how students are using all strategies when they read independently. Students love reading them and replying to them.

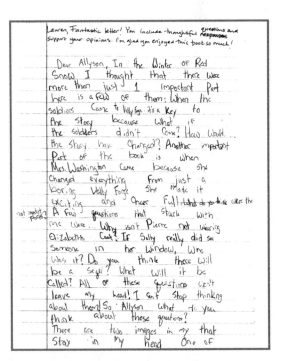

Group Thought Response: After the first meeting, Brendan's thinking didn't change. However, over time it did.

Book Group Letter: Lauren and Allyson discuss their thoughts on THE WINTER OF RED SNOW.

Concluding Thoughts

This cycle of planning, reading, and discussing continues until students complete the book. We continually listen in on groups and confer with individual readers. We address the needs as they arise. If we see a common struggle, we conduct a whole-group mini-lesson to deal with it.

As with all aspects of the curriculum, book groups improve with practice. We plan our year so that students are engaged in several book groups, giving them the opportunity to work with many classmates and read a variety of texts.

FINAL REFLECTION

We were moved to write this book because of our success in teaching reading strategies to students through focused studies. However, it was a humbling experience. Writing about how we teach caused us to examine closely our practice and make changes. Teaching is never static, and the lessons in this book represent only a slice of our teaching. We modify lessons based on past experience and the needs of our current students.

We hope this book provides a foundation on which you can build your own strategy studies that meet your style and the needs of your students. We hope that you will look to other teachers and to your students for ways to extend and deepen strategic reading. Thank you for visiting our classrooms.

Bibliography of Children's Books

Abbott, T. (1999). *Journey to the Volcano Palace*. New York: Scholastic, Inc.

Ada, A. (1995). *My Name Is Maria Isabel*. New York: Alladin Paperbacks.

Blume, J. (1971). *Freckle Juice*. New York: Dell Publishing.

Blume, J. (1974). *The Pain and the Great One*. Scarsdale, NY: Bradbury Press.

Brownlie, A. (1999). *Food and Festivals: West Africa*. Austin, TX: Raintree Steck-Vaughn.

Bulla, C.R. (1987). *The Chalk Box Kid*. New York: Random House.

Bunting, E. (1994). *Nasty Stinky Sneakers*. New York: HarperCollins.

Cameron, A. (1981). *The Stories Julian Tells*. New York: Pantheon Books.

Chukran, B. (2000). *Catch Me If You Can: The Road Runner*. Bothell, WA: Wright Group Books.

Clark, M. (1997). *A Treasury of Dragon Stories*. New York: Kingfisher.

Climo, S. (1996). *The Irish Cinderlad*. New York: HarperCollins.

- (1989). *The Egyptian Cinderella*. New York: HarperCollins.

Collier, J.L. and C.C. (1974). *My Brother Sam Is Dead*. New York: Four Winds Press.

- (1983). *War Comes to Willy Freeman*. New York: Delacorte.

Cosby, B. (1997). *The Meanest Thing to Say*. New York: Scholastic, Inc.

Craighead, J.G. (1972). *Julie of the Wolves*. New York: Harper & Row

Dahl, R. (1988). *James and the Giant Peach*. New York: Puffin Books.

Danziger, P. *Amber Brown* series. New York: Putnam.

Davis, L. (1998). *Dinosaur Dinners*. New York: DK Publishing, Inc.

DePaola, T. (1999). *26 Fairmount Avenue*. New York: Putnam

DiCamillo, K. (2000). *Because of Winn Dixie*. Cambridge, MA: Candlewick Press.

Du Bois, W.P. (1947). *The Twenty-One Balloons*. New York: The Viking Press.

Evans, D. (1996). *The Classroom at the End of the Hall*. New York: Scholastic, Inc.

Fleischman, P. (1980). *Half a Moon Inn*. HaperCollins: New York.

Fletcher, R. (1995). *Fig Pudding*. New York: Clarion Books

Fox, P. (1991). *Monkey Island*. New York: Orchard Press.

Gantos, J. (1994). *Heads or Tails: Stories from the Sixth Grade*. New York: Farrar Straus Giroux.

Gibbons, G. (2000). *Apples*. New York: Scholastic, Inc.

- (1999). *The Pumpkin Book*. New York: Scholastic, Inc

- (1993). *Spiders*. New York: Scholastic, Inc

Giff, P. R. (1984). *The Beast in Ms. Rooney's Room*. New York: Doubleday Books.

- (1998). *B-E-S-T Friends*. New York: Doubleday.

Goodman, J.E. (1998). *Hope's Crossing*. New York: Puffin Books.

Greenburg, D. *Zack Files* series. New York: Grosset and Dunlap.

Greenfield, E. (1978). *Honey, I Love*. New York: HarperCollins.

Haskings, J. (1987). *Counting Your Way Through Japan*. Minneapolis, MN: Carolrhoda Books.

Heinrichs, Ann. (1997). *A True Book Japan*. New York: Children's Press

Hesse, K. (1994). *Sable*. New York: Holt.

Howe, J. (1991). *Pinkey and Rex and the Spelling Bee*. New York: Scholastic, Inc.

Johns, L. (2000). *Animal Mix-Ups*. Bothell, WA: Twig Books

Juster, N. (1989). *The Phantom Tollbooth*. New York: Random House.

Kimmel, K.C. (1999). *Balto and the Great Race*. New York: Random House.

Krensky, S. *Lionel* series. New York: Dial Books for Young Readers.

Louie, A. (1982). *Yeh-Shen: A Cinderella Story from China*. New York: Philomel Books.

MacDonald, B.B. (1975). *Mrs. Piggle-Wiggle*. New York: HarperCollins.

Martin, R. (1992). *The Rough-Face Girl*. New York: G.P. Putnam's Sons.

McGovern, A. (1978). *Shark Lady: True Adventures of Eugenie Clark*. New York: Four Winds Press.

McLean, V.O. (1988). *Chasing the Moon to China*. Memphis, TN: Redbird Press.

Miles, Annie. (2000). *From Cow to Milk Carton*. Bothell, WA: Wright Group Books.

Minarik, E.H. *Little Bear* series. New York: Harper & Row

Munsch, R. (1997). *Alligator Baby*. New York: Scholastic, Inc.

Osborne, M. (1998). *Day of the Dragon*. New York: Random House.

- (1992). *Dinosaurs Before Dawn*. New York: Random House.

- (1995). *Night of the Ninjas*. New York: Random House.

Park, B. (1997). *Junie B. Jones Has a Monster Under Her Bed*. New York: Random House.

Park, T. (2000). *Taking your Camera to France*. Austin, TX: Raintree Steck-Vaughn Publishers.

Parsons, A. (1990). *Eyewitness Junior: Amazing Snakes*. New York: DK Publishing, Inc.

Patterson, F. (1987). *Koko's Story*. New York: Scholastic, Inc.

Perrault, C. (1988). *Cinderella*. New York: Knopf.

Pinkwater, D.M. (1976). *Lizard Music*. New York: Dodd, Mead.

Rylant, C. (1997). *The Blue Hill Meadows*. New York: Scholastic, Inc.

- (1998). *The Cobble Street Cousins*. New York: Aladdin Paperbacks.

San Souci, R.D. (1998). *Cendrillon: A Caribbean Cinderella*. New York: Simon and Schuster Books for Young Readers.

Scieszka, J. *Time Warp Trio* series. New York: Viking.

Smith, D. (1973). *A Taste of Blackberries*. New York: Scholastic, Inc.

Smith, R.K. (1984). *The War with Grandpa*. New York: Delacorte.

Spinelli, J. (1998). *Knots in My Yo-Yo String: The Autobiography of a Kid*. New York: Knopf.

- (2000). *Stargirl*. New York: Knopf

Steptoe, J. (1987). *Mufaro's Beautiful Daughters: An African Tale*. New York: Lothrop, Lee and Shepard Books.

Bibliography of Professional Resources

Baumann, J.F., Hoffman, J.V., Moon, J. and Duffy-Hester, A.M. (1998). "Where Are the Teachers' Voices in the Phonics/Whole Language Debate? Results for a Survey of U.S. Elementary Classroom Teachers." *The Reading Teacher* 51:636-650.

Braunger, J. and Lewis, J. (1997). *Building a Knowledge Base in Reading*. Newark, DE: International Reading Association.

Calkins, L. (2001). *The Art of Teaching Reading*. New York: Longman.

Cambourne, B. (1988). *The Whole Story: Natural Learning and the Acquisition of Literacy in the Classroom*. Ashton, Australia: Scholastic.

Cunningham, A.E., and Stanovich, K.E. (1998). "What Reading Does for the Mind." *American Educator* 21: 8-15.

Fountas, I. and Pinnell, G.S. (1996). *Guided Reading: Good First Teaching for All Children*. Portsmouth: Heinemann.

Harvey, S. and Goudvis, A. (2000). *Strategies That Work: Teaching Comprehension to Enhance Understanding*. York, ME: Stenhouse Books.

Keene, E.O. and Zimmermann, S. (1997). *Mosaic of Thought: Teaching Comprehension in a Reader's Workshop*. Portsmouth: Heinemann.

Mooney, M. (1990). *Reading To, With and By Children*. Katonah, NY: Richard C. Owen Publishers.

Pearson, D.P., Roehler, L.R., Dole, J.A. and Duffy, G.G. (1992). "Developing Expertise in Reading Comprehension." In *What Research Has to Say About Reading Instruction*, second edition. Eds. Samuels, J. and Farstrup, A. Newark, DE: International Reading Association.

Robb, L. (2000). *Teaching Reading in Middle School*. New York: Scholastic Professional Books.

Speigel, D.L. (1998). "Silver Bullets, Babies, and Bath Water: Literature Response Groups in a Balanced Literacy Program." *The Reading Teacher* 52: 114-124.

Strategy Study:

Week 1: Introduce

Day 1	Day 2	Day 3	Day 4	Day 5

Week 2: Extend

Day 6	Day 7	Day 8	Day 9	Day 10

Week 3: Deepen

Day 11	Day 12	Day 13	Day 14	Day 15

Week 4: Reflect on and Celebrate

Day 16	Day 17	Day 18	Day 19	Day 20

Name: _____ Date: _____

Story Map

Title: _____ Author: _____

Characters: _____

_____

_____

Setting: _____

_____

_____

Problem: _____

_____

_____

Solution: _____

_____

_____

Conclusion: _____

_____

_____

_____

Author's Message: _____

_____

_____

_____

On the back of this story map, draw the most important part of the story.

Teaching Comprehension Strategies All Readers Need   Scholastic Professional Books   An explanation of how to use this reproducible appears on page 26.

Name: _____   Date: _____

Nonfiction Reading Response Sheet

Title: _____   Author: _____

What is the main topic of your book?: _____

_____

_____

Draw a picture of a scene, story, or something you learned from your book:

After reading this book, name some facts you learned about the main topic that you didn't know beforehand.

_____

_____

_____

_____

_____

Name: _____ Date: _____

Connections T-Chart

Title: _____ Author: _____

Event in the Text	Connection

Teaching Comprehension Strategies All Readers Need Scholastic Professional Books An explanation of how to use this reproducible appears on page 48.

Name: _____ Date: _____

How Did Your Connections Help Your Comprehension?

Title: _____ Author: _____

Event	Connection

How did this connection help your comprehension?

Event	Connection

How did this connection help your comprehension?

Event	Connection

How did this connection help your comprehension?

Name:_____   Date:_____

Use Connections
To Ask Good Questions

Title:_____   Author:_____

Connection	Question

Answers to the Question

Connection	Question

Answers to the Question

Connection	Question

Answers to the Question

Teaching Comprehension Strategies All Readers Need   *Scholastic Professional Books*   An explanation of how to use this reproducible appears on page 50.

Name: _____ Date: _____

Prediction T-Chart

Title: _____ Author: _____

Prediction With Support	Outcome With Support

Name: _____ Date: _____

Update Predictions

Title: _____ Author: _____

Prediction	Outcome	Updated Prediction

Teaching Comprehension Strategies All Readers Need   Scholastic Professional Books   An explanation of how to use this reproducible appears on page 62.

Name: _____

Date: _____

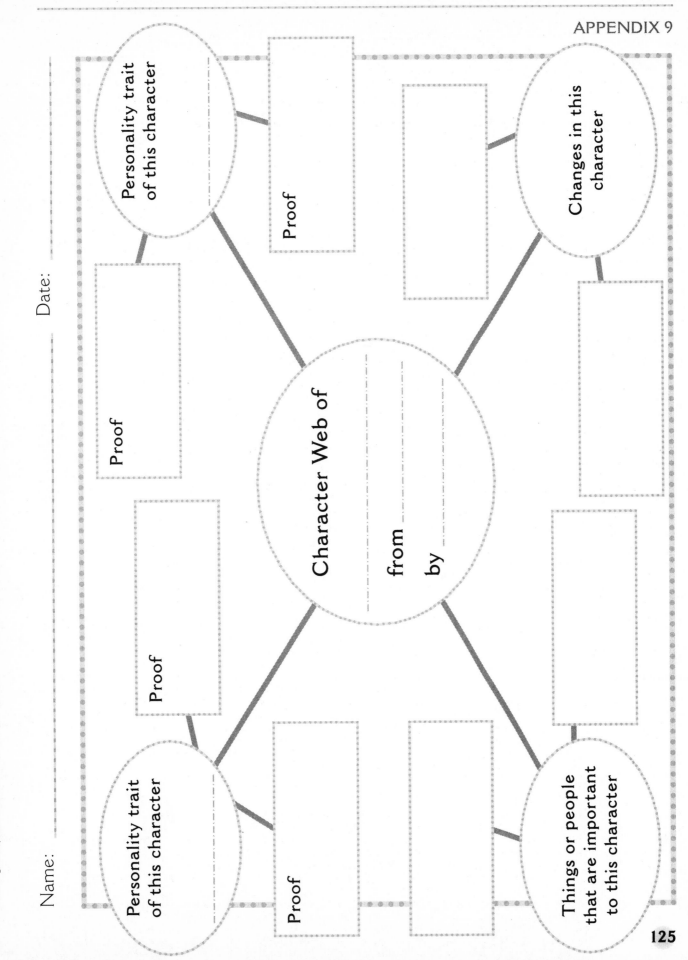

Personality trait of this character

Proof

Changes in this character

Proof

Proof

Character Web of _____

from _____

by _____

Personality trait of this character

Proof

Things or people that are important to this character

Name: _____   Date: _____

Big Idea T-Chart

Title: _____   Author: _____

Big Idea	Details That Support It

Name: _____   Date: _____

Book Group Plan

Group Members: _____

Author: _____

Your group will meet every other day. What will members expect of one another?

How many pages will each member read between meetings? _____

What sort of documentation should members bring to the group?

What happens if a member comes unprepared?

How will you conduct your discussion? Each member needs to be involved.

At the end of the meeting, each member should write a brief reflection on how talking about the book changed his or her understanding of the book.

Response Sheet

Name: _____ Date: _____

Title: _____

Date Begun: _____ Completed: _____

Page	Date	Code	What are you thinking as you read?

Codes:

C = Connection
BI = Big Idea
DU = Part that isn't Understood

P = Prediction
ID = Important Details
MP = Mind Picture

V = Unknown Vocabulary
?B, ?D, ?A = Questions Before, During and After Reading

Teaching Comprehension Strategies All Readers Need   Scholastic Professional Books   An explanation of how to use this reproducible appears on page 109.